LESLIE KAREN NELSON

GIVING, *Recklessly*

*Testimonials and examples
to inspire higher levels of generosity*

Trilogy Christian Publishers
A Wholly Owned Subsidiary of Trinity Broadcasting Network
2442 Michelle Drive
Tustin, CA 92780
Copyright © 2024 by Leslie Karen Nelson
All Scripture quotations, unless otherwise noted, are taken from the Holy Bible, New Living Translation, copyright © 1996, 2004, 2015 by Tyndale House Foundation. Used by permission of Tyndale House Publishers, Inc., Carol Stream, Illinois 60188. All rights reserved.
All rights reserved, including the right to reproduce this book or portions thereof in any form whatsoever.
For information, address Trilogy Christian Publishing
Rights Department, 2442 Michelle Drive, Tustin, CA 92780.
Trilogy Christian Publishing/ TBN and colophon are trademarks of Trinity Broadcasting Network.
For information about special discounts for bulk purchases, please contact Trilogy Christian Publishing.

Trilogy Disclaimer: The views and content expressed in this book are those of the author and may not necessarily reflect the views and doctrine of Trilogy Christian Publishing or the Trinity Broadcasting Network.

10 9 8 7 6 5 4 3 2 1
Library of Congress Cataloging-in-Publication Data is available.
ISBN 979-8-89333-434-0
ISBN 979-8-89333-435-7 (ebook)

DEDICATION

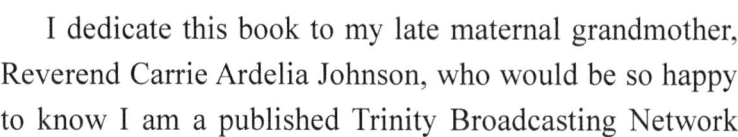

I dedicate this book to my late maternal grandmother, Reverend Carrie Ardelia Johnson, who would be so happy to know I am a published Trinity Broadcasting Network author.

During the latter years of her life especially, I remember visiting Nanny whenever my immediate family's military reassignments and vacations allowed us to return to my hometown of Philadelphia, Pennsylvania. I made those visits with her a priority. Nanny would sit in her pale blue striped recliner, positioned in the corner of her living room, listening to TBN either on the radio or television. At the same time, she carried on conversations with us. As she spoke or laughed, she mostly leaned her head to the left side and framed her thumb and index finger around the eyeglass lens over her left eye. Many years earlier, she had completely lost the use of her right eye. As she was largely confined to her home due to age and disability, I believe the TBN sermons and programs brought her comfort and companionship when she was alone, a constant connection to the thriving Christian faith she clung to amid her circumstances.

The last time I visited Nanny in her home before her death was late November 1995. To this day, I vividly recall feeling impatient, overheated, and nauseous as I stood in her small, cramped yellow kitchen in North Philadelphia reheating her prepared Thanksgiving meal. I was pregnant with my fourth child and was experiencing the associated discomfort of the first trimester. Nonetheless, I deeply regret rushing through that last visit with her, and the memory is still fresh over twenty-eight years later. Also fresh are the deep love I always felt for her and how grateful I am for the faith, honesty, and self-discipline she instilled in my and my mother's lives.

My dear unforgettable Nanny, continue to rest in peace. This one's for you.

My grandmother, Reverend Carrie Ardelia Johnson, sitting in her favorite chair.

FOREWORD

In a world often consumed by self-interest and personal gain, Leslie K. Nelson's *Giving, Recklessly* serves as a beacon of light, illuminating the transformative power of selfless giving. Through heartfelt testimonies and vivid examples, Nelson navigates the depths of human generosity, inspiring readers to embrace a mindset of abundance and compassion.

From the poignant dedication to her late grandmother, Reverend Carrie Ardelia Johnson, whose unwavering faith and love laid the foundation for Nelson's own journey, to the candid acknowledgments of the pivotal individuals who shaped her life, Nelson's narrative is imbued with gratitude and reverence. Each page resonates with the profound impact of giving, whether it be through acts of kindness, hospitality, mentorship, or enduring friendships.

Nelson's exploration extends beyond the tangible manifestations of generosity, delving into the spiritual dimensions of giving. Drawing upon biblical wisdom and personal reflections, she uncovers the divine essence of giving, portraying it not merely as a gesture of charity but as a sacred calling bestowed upon humanity. Through the lens of faith, Nelson invites readers to embrace their inherent capacity to serve others, echoing the timeless admonition to steward God's grace with fidelity and devotion.

As Nelson delves into the biblical narratives of creation, crucifixion, and salvation, she illuminates the profound truth that giving lies at the heart of the Christian faith. Just as God lavishly bestows His love and grace upon humanity, Nelson implores readers to emulate this extravagant generosity in their own lives, becoming vessels of compassion and instruments of God's boundless love.

In *Giving, Recklessly* Leslie K. Nelson beckons us to transcend the confines of self-interest and embark on a journey of radical generosity. With eloquence and sincerity, she reminds us that true fulfillment is found not in the accumulation of wealth or status but in the joy of giving and the richness of human connection. This book is a testament to the enduring power of generosity to transform lives, illuminate hearts, and usher in a brighter, more compassionate world.

– Pastor Daniel Gray,
Lead Pastor, Chapelhill Church, Douglasville, Georgia

PREFACE

When I began drafting this book, I knew I wanted to talk about how and why helping others has impacted my life. I also wanted to inspire and applaud those who selflessly give their time, talents, or resources over and over without expecting anything in return. Then I wanted to reach some who might feel bitter or used up from giving to others because their efforts are not yielding the desired outcomes. Most importantly, I needed to share and testify about the ultimate Act of giving by my Lord and Savior Jesus Christ and provide biblical examples of people God used to save the lost.

I thought about calling the book something creative like "The Art of Helping." However, a quick online search revealed multiple books by that title, and I frankly did not find researching copyrights a beneficial use of my time and energy.

"Giving" was a close enough substitute for helping, but that still was not enough. I felt compelled to use words that have meanings beyond the *natural* because I believe desiring to help others, without pretentiousness or aiming for personal glory, is a deeply rooted gift from a *supernatural* God.

According to Trinity Family Wealth Advisors, there are seven forms of generosity: "thoughts, words, money, time, things, influence, and attention."[1] I wholeheartedly agree with these seven broad forms of generosity. However, by extension and from my own firsthand experiences, generosity can further manifest itself in these six ways: kindness, hospitality, mentorship, candor, belongingness, and enduring friendships. There is certainly not a finite list because there are countless nuances and levels of need. We also know that giving can overlap in multiple ways, such as when one provides both hospitality and sustenance to others. This book provides inspirational, true accounts of the seven specific manifestations I have either experienced or learned about through others, allowing us to envision or identify a wider range of giving possibilities.

Having defined giving, I was still searching for another word to describe the nature and extent of what I know is my spiritual gift. That is when the Holy Spirit dropped "reckless" in my head.

Now, I would not necessarily characterize all the situations when I have helped others as reckless giving, but each that I will describe in this book is certainly memorable. For as long as I can recall, people have given to me recklessly too. So I also hope to give due credit to those generous people because even without them knowing God's plan, He allowed me to experience those situations and retain the memories that, in turn, created a passion within me to help others. Finally, as I wrote this book,

God pointed me to friends, family members, and new acquaintances who had also received gifts from generous people; they were more than happy to share their stories and pay tribute to those kind people.

Admittedly, by some standards my giving is reckless, but I submit that those natural tendencies separate a true spiritual gift or calling from a forced, trite, or random act of kindness. 1 Peter 4:10 NLT leaves no room for debate with this command: *"God has given each of you a gift from his great variety of spiritual gifts. Use them well to serve one another."*

Then there is Luke 16:10–12 in which the physician Luke says,

> *If you are faithful in little things, you will be faithful in large ones. But if you are dishonest in little things, you won't be honest with greater responsibilities. And if you are untrustworthy about worldly wealth, who will trust you with the true riches of heaven? And if you are not faithful with other people's things, why should you be trusted with things of your own?*

Also consider Psalm 139:3, which says, *"You see me when I travel and when I rest at home. You know everything I do."*

I am neither ashamed nor apologetic about my gift of giving and how God has ordered my steps. God, I stand ready to be trusted with big things when it comes to helping others.

ACKNOWLEDGMENTS

This is my first published book. For as long as I can remember, I have done some combination of journaling, writing our family's Christmas letters, or sending inspirational notes to people going through tough situations. Many times I would jump up in the middle of a restless night of sleep, full of thoughts that I had to write down immediately. As I reflect on my passion for writing, I realize the common denominator in all these scenarios has been the need to express the richness of my life, as I define it, and to encourage and share with the people I am blessed to call family and friends.

First and foremost, I thank God for loving me unconditionally and giving me the vision to write this book. He dropped words and scenarios in my head at the oddest times. When I think about the chapter you will read entitled "By Design or Coincidence," I am amazed at the seemingly coincidental situations I encountered that aligned with the theme of reckless giving. Likewise, I truly believe God ordered my everyday ordinary life so it would be a testimonial for others to see, and begin to trust in, His abundant love for all of us. I have learned He never does anything by accident!

Without my husband, David, I would never have

experienced such a rich earthly adult life. Rich in the sense of having many highs and lows that shaped me into who I am. I thank my husband for our marriage and for the really important things we always agreed on—like our mutual commitment to raising our four children well and caring for our immediate families as best as possible.

Demetrius, Tiffany, Kiana, and Mikhala are amazing. Not only did our four children endure the highs and lows of military life, but they also grew into resilient, determined, and loving adults who are impacting the world one person and one experience at a time. I am in awe of our individual and collective relationships and the fact that we stay connected despite geography, busyness, or differences in opinions. I feel their love and respect daily and count it all joy that we are not only family but also friends.

In 2012 my husband and I were blessed to add to our family's numbers a son-in-law, Jason Ellis Hooten Alexander. While the main person God blessed is his wife and our daughter, Tiffany, I am in awe of how Jason weaved his way into the hearts of the rest of our immediate family too. He jokingly calls me "Millie," which is short for mother-in-law, so I, in turn, call him "Sillie," which is short for son-in-law. I have watched Jason and Tiffany grow stronger together over the past twelve years as they eliminated their student loan debt, launched a small business, coached young adults, and pursued other important family and career objectives. In addition to having Christ in their lives, I know their successes were all the more attainable because Jason accepted the biblical charge to lead his family from the very beginning of their marriage. In 2023 he also became the executive pastor of their church—Mosaic Church in Mableton, Georgia. I want to acknowledge the very special person Jason is while also thanking God for His wisdom in knowing who, in the natural form, would love and care for our daughter best.

You will read about my parents and my early life of material lack in this book; however, none of what I describe about their relationship and my upbringing detracts from my overwhelming love for both. My dad, Jerome Rogers, died in August 2021. I still miss him every single day. He gave me my laugh, my sense of humor, my big nose, and my love for tasty food. Walking outdoors was his passion and is mine too. Talk about giving! God blessed me to care for my dad in the final five years of his life, after only seeing him occasionally over the previous thirty-four years. During one of our final months together, we took a long walk through a local park in Sterling, Virginia. I vividly recall how determined he was to complete that walk—even as we realized we had not carried any water to refresh ourselves along the way. Our big chuckle for that day was having to ask various softball teams on the field if they could spare a bottle or two, and we were certainly willing to pay! Memories of who he was when we were together are forever etched in my mind, and I am deeply grateful for being able to serve and love him during his final years of life.

My mom, Marion Rogers, is a rock. She taught me about faith, resilience, courage, and hope. She kept going when others might have succumbed to the burdens of poverty and the oxymoron of single parenting while married. I and my three siblings sat in front-row seats watching her when the going got tough, as she literally and metaphorically dropped to her knees, yielded to God's divine power, and then clawed her way out of the darkness of poverty and other societal encumbrances. During the last eight years of my immediate family's military service, my mom relocated with us to help care for our four children, and yes, she still imparts her wisdom to them today whenever there is an opportunity. At the age of eighty-four, she is still my "shero" and my ultimate human role model.

For the record, I have the best sister and two brothers ever. Glenn Rogers, Allener Baker-Rogers, and Michael Rogers, you have been lifelong inspirations. I always wanted my own four children to enjoy their sibling relationships as much as the four of us still do. I cannot thank you enough for loving this one sister (with the very uncommon birthday) as you have.

An additional special thanks to my sister, Allener, who became my accountability partner for this book. She read draft chapters, gave me critical feedback, and shared her experiences as a published author. She was also patient with me when I did not meet deadlines for reviewing excerpts for the book she is currently writing. In short, she kept me level-headed as I treaded this new territory called authorship. We also had a candid, heartfelt conversation just before I submitted my book manuscript in which we reflected on the various forms of giving we experienced not only in our childhood but also in our adult lives. As she so accurately recalled, the four siblings' willingness to forgive and help each other over the years, despite differences in opinion, beliefs, and other relationship challenges, has been priceless. It is all coming together, my sister; this will be yet another year to realize new dreams and to experience some pretty remarkable blessings in the process.

I also want to thank everyone who allowed me to use real names as I shared their stories in this book. Doing so made the experiences all the more memorable and relatable. In those instances where I was unable to get permission, out of respect and to preserve their confidentiality I have used fictitious names instead. I am amazed at how my relationships with you or your own special experiences fit into my overall story of giving, recklessly. I encourage you to reflect on your gifts of giving as well as those extended to you and then continue to pay it forward. Receive the call the Lord declared over Abram too: *"I will make you into a great nation. I will bless you and make you famous, and you will be a blessing to others"* (Genesis 12:2).

Finally, there is simply not enough space and time for me to acknowledge all my longstanding, influential, special friends. Suffice it to say, I treasure my sisters from other misters, and my brothers from other mothers. I have loved and been supported by you—my intimate circle of friends—when my own biological family lived both near and far away. David and I trusted you to help raise and encourage our children, and we still remember and celebrate that entire journey with you. I also have not forgotten that several of you encouraged me to keep writing, and this book reflects your support and belief in what God eventually called me to do. My special friends—you know who you are, and I love you to the moon and back.

My parents, Jerome and Marion Rogers, at my daughter Tiffany's wedding in 2012.

INTRODUCTION

This book is divided into three parts
with three appendices.

Part 1 – Biblical Perspective contains three chapters about God's consummate giving and four examples of biblical characters who gave recklessly to others during their time on this earth.

Part 2 – Personal Perspective and Experiences contains six chapters that provide general accounts and observations about giving.

Part 3 – Seven Specific Gifts of Giving contains seven chapters with testimonials and real-life examples of the gifts of kindness; hospitality; care, encouragement, and mentorship; candor; belongingness; time; and enduring friendships.

Appendix 1 provides additional biblical Scriptures and quotes.

Appendix 2 provides additional references and resources.

Appendix 3 provides a timeline of our family's military reassignments and/or significant events.

TABLE OF CONTENTS

Dedication 5

Foreword 7

Preface 9

Acknowledgments 13

Introduction 19

Part 1: Biblical Perspective

Chapter 1: God's Extreme Benevolence 25

Chapter 2: Our Prodigal Father Unpacked 33

Chapter 3: Four Biblical Examples 39

Part 2: Personal Perspective And Experiences

Chapter 4: Digging Deeper into "Reckless" 49

Chapter 5: On the Receiving End of Giving 53

Chapter 6: By Design or Coincidence? 65

Chapter 7: When the Blessings Override
the Prognosis 77

Chapter 8: The Blessing of Having
Resilient Children 85

Chapter 9: When Saying "No" is Beneficial 95

Part 3: Seven Specific Gifts Of Giving

Chapter 10: The Gift of Random
Acts of Kindness............................ 101

Chapter 11: The Gift of Hospitality—Roxie....... 111

Chapter 12: The Gifts of Care, Encouragement,
and Mentorship............................ 117

Chapter 13: The Gift of Candor—David and Jacqui 131

Chapter 14: The Gift of Belongingness—
Ida and Jaida.............................. 139

Chapter 15: The Gift of Time—Kimberly 147

Chapter 16: The Gift of Enduring Friendships..... 151

Epilogue 175

Appendix 1: Additional Biblical Scriptures and Quotes.. 179

Appendix 2: Additional References and Resources 183

Appendix 3: Our Military Assignments and/or Significant
Events Timeline 185

Endnotes 187

PART 1

Biblical Perspective

CHAPTER 1:
GOD'S EXTREME BENEVOLENCE

The Bible is replete with examples of God's extreme benevolence, beginning with His creation of the heavens and the earth, to Jesus's crucifixion on the cross, and to His promise of eternal life to those who love Him and keep His commands. Let's explore various Scriptures about giving that form the foundation of our Christian faith:

Creation

> *Genesis 1:1: "In the beginning, God created the heavens and the earth."* To the dark, desolate, and formless heavens and earth that He chose to create, God brought light, beauty, structure, and hope.
>
> *Genesis 1:26: "Then God said, "Let us make human beings in our image, to be like us. They will reign over the fish in the sea, the*

birds in the sky, the livestock, all the wild animals on the earth, and the small animals that scurry along the ground." In a land bereft of human life, activity, and direction, God chose to create males and females to reproduce, subdue, and lead.

Colossians 1:16: "For through him God created everything in the heavenly realms and on earth. He made the things we can see and the things we can't see—such as thrones, kingdoms, rulers, and authorities in the unseen world. Everything was created through him and for him." As much as we have acquired, discovered, and invented, this Scripture is a stark reminder that, without God, nothing we do as humans is possible.

The Crucifixion

Isaiah 53:7–11:

He was oppressed and treated harshly, yet he never said a word. He was led like a lamb to the slaughter. And as a sheep is silent before the shearers, he did not open his mouth. Unjustly condemned, he was led away. No one cared that he died without descendants, that his life was cut short in midstream. But he was struck down for the rebellion of my people. He had done no wrong and had never deceived anyone. But he was buried like a criminal; he was put in a rich man's grave. But it was the LORD's good plan to crush him and cause him grief. Yet when his life is made an offering for sin, he will have many descendants. He will enjoy a long life, and the LORD's good plan will prosper in his hands. When he sees all that is accomplished by his anguish, he will be satisfied. And because of his experience, my righteous servant will make it possible for many to be counted righteous, for he will bear all their sins.

Luke 22:42: "Father, if you are willing, please take this cup of suffering away from me. Yet I want your will to be done, not mine." Despite the ridicule, physical pain, and mental torture, Jesus paid the ultimate sacrifice for the redemption of our sins.

2 Corinthians 5:21: "For God made Christ, who never sinned, to be the offering for our sin, so that we could be made right with God through Christ."

Salvation

John 3:16: "For this is how God loved the world: He gave his one and only Son, so that

> *everyone who believes in him will not perish but have eternal life."*

Romans 5:15–18:

> *But there is a great difference between Adam's sin and God's gracious gift. For the sin of this one man, Adam, brought death to many. But even greater is God's wonderful grace and his gift of forgiveness to many through this other man, Jesus Christ. And the result of God's gracious gift is very different from the result of that one man's sin. For Adam's sin led to condemnation, but God's free gift leads to our being made right with God, even though we are guilty of many sins. For the sin of this one man, Adam, caused death to rule over many. But even greater is God's wonderful grace and his gift of righteousness, for all who receive it will live in triumph over sin and death through this one man, Jesus Christ. Yes, Adam's one sin brings condemnation for everyone, but Christ's one act of righteousness brings a right relationship with God and new life for everyone.*

> *Romans 6:23: "For the wages of sin is death, but the free gift of God is eternal life through Christ Jesus our LORD."*

Galatians 2:20: "*My old self has been crucified with Christ. It is no longer I who live, but Christ lives in me. So I live in this earthly body by trusting in the Son of God, who loved me and gave himself for me.*"

Ephesians 2:4–5: "*But God is so rich in mercy, and he loved us so much, that even though we were dead because of our sins, he gave us life when he raised Christ from the dead. (It is only by God's grace that you have been saved!)*"

Ephesians 2:8–9: "*God saved you by his grace when you believed. And you can't take credit for this; it is a gift from God. Salvation is not a reward for the good things we have done, so none of us can boast about it.*"

The Holy Spirit

Luke 11:11–13: "*You fathers—if your children ask for a fish, do you give them a snake instead? Or if they ask for an egg, do you give them a scorpion? Of course not! So if you sinful people know how to give good gifts to your children, how much more will your heavenly Father give the Holy Spirit to those who ask him.*"

Galatians 5:22–23: "*But the Holy Spirit produces this kind of fruit in our lives: love, joy, peace, patience, kindness, goodness, faithfulness, gentleness, and self-control. There is no law against these things!*"

Provision and Hope for the Future

Deuteronomy 28:12: "*The LORD will send rain at the proper time from his rich treasury in the heavens and will bless all the work you do. You will lend to many nations, but you will never need to borrow from them.*"

Isaiah 54:17: "*But in that coming day no weapon turned against you will succeed. You will silence every voice raised up to accuse you. These benefits are enjoyed by the servants of the LORD; their vindication will come from me. I, the LORD, have spoken!*"

Jeremiah 29:11: "*'For I know the plans I have for you,' says the LORD. 'They are plans for good and not for disaster, to give you a future and a hope.'*" As long as I am breathing, I have full confidence that He has a plan for me.

Matthew 6:33: *"Seek the Kingdom of God above all else, and live righteously, and he will give you everything you need."*

CHAPTER 2:
OUR PRODIGAL FATHER UNPACKED

One day my good friend Christina Conley told me about a book she was reading called *The Prodigal God*.[2] At the time, she was honing in on late author Timothy Keller's strategic placement of the definition of "prodigal" in his Introduction. As Keller cited, Merriam-Webster's Collegiate Dictionary defined the adjective as "recklessly spendthrift," or spending until you have nothing left.

As my friend suspected would happen, at that point I was drawn to Keller's book—hook, line, and sinker as they say—because the definition validated my belief that we should never stop giving. From that day forward, I could not put the book down as Keller also unpacked an angle of God's generosity that completely escaped me during the countless times I have read the Parable of the Prodigal Son (Luke 15:11–32). I also want to thank Pastor Daniel Gray, who gave me even more clarity about this parable through a sermon he preached at Chapel Hill Church in Douglasville,

Georgia, in 2023.

You see, God is like the father in the parable. He forgives us of our sins even when we disregard or turn away from the abundant blessings He provides. And, when we come to our end, disgusted with our decisions, failures, and the wrong choices we might make, God is always there to receive us back. When we feel that He is distant, He is still there waiting, watching, and ready to run and meet us wherever we are. Distance is not a factor either, because God is omnipresent—He is everywhere. While, like the Prodigal Son, we might not feel worthy, the Father never thinks of our relationship with Him that way. Our sin does not change anything. We have our Father's blood, likeness, and love—period!!!

The Prodigal Son's father also observed his other son's bitterness and resentment. Like God, he would have generously forgiven that son too had he not been so entrenched in self-righteousness—as if satisfying a list of Pharisaical rules like he had done should have disqualified the Prodigal Son (his brother) from experiencing their father's unconditional love.

My understanding of the parable got even deeper one Sunday in October 2023, when a visiting pastor preached a sermon at our church entitled "What Really Matters." The sermon reminded me again about God's unconditional love and the opportunity for salvation that He gives to everyone equally. The pastor's imperative was not only to pray for those who do not know Jesus, but also to remember three things: people matter, the way we live matters, and eternity matters.

People Matter

Because our timing is different from God's, He is patient in so many ways. He is a loving God, One who desires that everyone live and ultimately come to repentance (2 Peter 3:8–9). To fulfill His desire, He longs for Christians to step out of their comfort zone and have an open heart to share their faith with others—without fear because "perfect love expels all fear" (1 John 4:18). The brother of the Prodigal Son was so entrenched in how *he* felt, how undervalued *he* felt, and how much attention his brother received that he neglected to remember that every person matters—even one who has walked away and marred the family's reputation.

The Way We Live Matters

In 2 Peter 3:11–12, the apostle Peter implores Christians to live holy and Godly lives since we do not know when the heavens and earth will be destroyed. This Scripture is so powerful, and it always reminds me of a song I sang at summer camp in the 1970s called "They'll Know We Are Christians."[3] Back then, I did not know Fr. Peter Scholtes, a Catholic priest, wrote this Christian hymn in the 1960s, but the words resonate as much with me today as they did over forty years ago:

"We will walk with each other, we will walk hand in hand; We will walk with each other, we will walk hand in hand; And together we'll spread the news that God is in our land. And they'll know we are Christians by our love, by our love, yes, they'll know we are Christians by our love."

The brother of the Prodigal Son missed this critical point too. His time spent anguishing over his father's perceived favoritism could have been better spent by honoring his father and doing God's will with a pure heart. Instead, the brother functioned with malintent—always trying to one-up the younger brother and earn rewards with a carnal set of rules.

Eternity Matters

"And just as each person is destined to die once and after that comes judgment, so also Christ was offered once for all time as a sacrifice to take away the sins of many people. He will come again, not to deal with our sins, but to bring salvation to all who are eagerly waiting for him." (Hebrews 9:27–28)

It does not matter whether our death occurs by natural causes, accident, illness, malice, or a self-inflicted manner—each of us has a limited time to live. And while the grief we experience after the loss of a loved one is often devastating and prolonged, as Christians we also believe that there is a much greater reward in eternity. So when the pastor also asked the congregation whether we have been successful in the things that matter, the proverbial light bulb turned on, and we were compelled to re-evaluate our intentionality. You see, only eternal things will remain. Not wealth gained or lost, high-profile careers, fancy cars, or even the number of livestock the other brother acquired in the Prodigal Son parable. We have to fix our sights on heaven and an eternity that is beyond what we can ever think or imagine (Revelation 7).

Even if you decide not to buy Keller's book, I hope I have piqued your curiosity enough to dig deeper into the meaning of this parable and how it applies to your walk with Christ.

CHAPTER 3:

FOUR BIBLICAL EXAMPLES

"Go the extra mile for someone today. Help someone who could use a hand."
— **Fellowship of Christian Athletes**

Example 1: The Rebekah Principle

Genesis 24 tells us of Abraham's desire to find a suitable wife for his son Isaac, someone not from the daughters of the Canaanites in Canaan where he lived but from his own country, Ur of the Chaldeans, and of his own relatives. Abraham sent his senior household servant to find such a woman and also implored the servant to take an oath that he would not take Isaac back to Abraham's native country. However, the servant would be released from the oath if the woman refused to relocate to Canaan.

On the evening of the servant's arrival outside of the town where Abraham's brother, Nahor, lived, he decided to rest temporarily near a well where the town's women frequented to draw water. Laden with ten of Abraham's camels that carried loads of many good things, the servant earnestly prayed to encounter a young woman who met certain criteria: *"This is my request. I will ask one of them, 'Please give me a drink from your jug.' If she says, 'Yes, have a drink, and I will water your camels, too!'—let her be the one you have selected as Isaac's wife. This is how I will know that you have shown unfailing love to my master"* (Genesis 24:14). It came to pass that Rebekah, Abraham's relative through Nahor, appeared even before the servant finished praying, and she responded exactly according to his request. However, Rebekah's generosity did not stop there. When the servant also asked whether there was room at her father's house for him, his men, and the camel to spend the night, without hesitation Rebekah offered a room for him as well as "plenty of straw and fodder" for the camel.

But here is the icing on the cake. Abraham's servant knew by then that Rebekah was the answer to his master's prayer, and that the Lord ordained her to return to Canaan to become Isaac's wife. While her family also consented, they sought to detain her for ten days or so. However, when asked, Rebekah expressed no hesitation about leaving right away: *"And she replied, 'Yes, I will go'"* (Genesis 24:58). And oh, what a love story it was! As the troupe headed back toward Canaan, Isaac and Rebekah laid eyes on each other, and it was love at first sight. Rebekah had gone the extra mile to help someone, and that decision brought

FOUR BIBLICAL EXAMPLES

God's favor to her, Abraham, his master servant, and a host of generations.

Example 2: The Good Samaritan

We learn in Luke 10:25–37 that Jesus had an uncanny knack for teaching when He walked the earth, particularly with the Pharisees who constantly looked for ways to trip Him up. On one particular occasion when an expert in the law questioned how he could have eternal life, Jesus instructed him, *"Love your neighbor as yourself."* Because the expert simply could not allow Jesus to have the final word, he doggedly asked Jesus to further explain who would be considered his neighbor. And so the parable of The Good Samaritan unfolded.

> *Jesus replied with a story: "A Jewish man was traveling from Jerusalem down to Jericho, and he was attacked by bandits. They stripped him of his clothes, beat him up, and left him half dead beside the road. By chance a priest came along. But when he saw the man lying there, he crossed to the other side of the road and passed him by. A Temple assistant walked over and looked at him lying there, but he also passed by on the other side. Then a despised Samaritan came along, and when he saw the man, he felt compassion for him. Going over to him, the Samaritan soothed his wounds with olive oil and wine and bandaged*

> *them. Then he put the man on his own donkey and took him to an inn, where he took care of him. The next day he handed the innkeeper two silver coins, telling him, 'Take care of this man. If his bill runs higher than this, I'll pay you the next time I'm here.' Now which of these three would you say was a neighbor to the man who was attacked by bandits?" Jesus asked. The man replied, "The one who showed him mercy." Then Jesus said, "Yes, now go and do the same." (Luke 10:30–37)*

The lesson of the Good Samaritan is clear: when faced with opportunities to help people in dire need, we too should choose the path of giving beyond worldly expectations.

Example 3: Esther

One of many examples of God's interventions to save the Jews is recounted in the Book of Esther. The story is also yet another example of how God places His people in certain positions to achieve His divine purpose.

Imagine a wife in biblical times, Queen Vashti, who disobeyed the king's command to appear before a huge celebratory banquet to showcase her beauty. Not only was her disobedience embarrassing, but it also set a dangerous precedence that other wives might follow should King Xerxes not be able to save face. Upon the advice of his closest wise men, an extensive search ensued to find a wife to replace Queen Vashti.

Despite being an orphan, the young and beautiful Esther had been raised by her concerned and wise cousin, Mordecai. It was God's favor that intervened at this point, as Esther became the recipient of such favor in the form of special food and extensive beauty treatments that King Xerxes ultimately selected her to be the new queen, replacing Vashti. However, she and Mordecai both lived with the secret of being Jewish—a background and nationality that surely would have excluded her from royalty had it been known.

Once again, God was in the mix, placing Mordecai in a location where he overheard a plot to kill King Xerxes. After passing on this information to his surrogate daughter, Queen Esther, she was able to report the conspiracy and credit Mordecai. Although unknown at the time, Mordecai's actions would also help him become a credible source of information when the evil, dishonest noble, Haman, plotted to kill all the Jews to camouflage his true hate for the insubordinate Mordecai.

Using her wisdom and influence, Esther courageously went before King Xerxes after Mordecai convinced her of Haman's manipulation of the king's decree that led to the death of many Jews. Her actions were ultimately a gift to God's people and yet another confirmation of His love for them.

Example 4: Joseph

Joseph is probably best known for being that brother whom his siblings loved to hate. After all, as we learn in Genesis 37, his aged father Jacob made it clear that he loved Joseph more by giving him a very expensive and lavish robe. To add salt to the proverbial wound, Joseph dared to share a dream with his brothers that was properly interpreted to mean that Joseph would one day reign over them. When Joseph went even further to share another dream that signified that his parents and brothers would one day bow down to him, their jealousy and contempt for him increased exponentially.

As the story goes, the brothers initially plotted to kill Joseph, but they ultimately sold him into slavery. They had no way of knowing that the very same act would lead to the prophetic fulfillment of Joseph's dream. While I encourage you to read the entire story, here are seven ways God extended His gifts of mercy and protection to Joseph:

1. God used Joseph's brother, Reuben, to protect Joseph by sidetracking the brothers from their initial plan to kill him. (Genesis 37:19–23)

2. God divinely directed a caravan of Israelites, who were en route to Egypt, to come across the brothers as they plotted Joseph's fate. (Genesis 37:25–28)

3. Inexplicably, Joseph found favor in the eyes of his Egyptian master, Potiphar, which led to

him assuming a high position in that household. (Genesis 39:1–6a)

4. God granted Joseph the wisdom, courage, and integrity to avoid an adulterous relationship with Potiphar's wife. While her accusations still led to his imprisonment, Joseph continued to honor God by his words and actions. (Genesis 39:6b–20)

5. While imprisoned, God saw to it that Joseph earned the favor of the prison warden. Once again, Joseph was elevated to a high position and put in charge of all the other prisoners. (Genesis 39:21–23)

6. After a lengthy imprisonment, Joseph was released and went on to become Pharaoh's second in command. This stature positioned Joseph to save many people, which ultimately demonstrated more of God's protection over His people. (Genesis 40:23—41:57)

7. God ultimately reunited Joseph with his father and brothers. (Genesis 45)

PART 2

Personal Perspective And Experiences

CHAPTER 4:

DIGGING DEEPER INTO "RECKLESS"

In his 2018 post "Reckless Giving,"[4] John W. Fischer reminds his readers of the biblical precedence for giving, recklessly. As the phrase conveys, reckless giving should not make sense to the average person. In fact, to others, a reckless giver might seem foolish or naïve. In my lifetime, I have certainly received my fair share of comments from others along those lines.

For Christians, giving should be a natural extension and expression of our belief in and obedience to God. The physician, Luke, implored the spiritually lost Theophilus and Christians today, *"Give, and you will receive. Your gift will return to you in full—pressed down, shaken together to make room for more, running over, and poured into your lap. The amount you give will determine the amount you get back"* (Luke 6:38). C.S. Lewis also said it well: "I do not believe one can settle how much we ought to give. I am afraid the only safe rule is to give more than we can spare …"[5]

Fischer also suggests that giving should feel like the sensation of a wild Disneyland ride—where we are both exhilarated and light-headed from the experience. Frankly, I am terrified by the mere thought of riding a roller coaster that haphazardly whips people around curves, slowly ascends to a high peak, and then plummets toward the ground at a bizarre rate of speed that leaves its riders breathless. However, from my experiences with giving to others, the excitement and sometimes emotional response that comes from knowing you have potentially redirected someone around one of life's metaphorical curves, or given someone a renewed and elevated hope, is like no other. This particular fulfillment I get from selfless giving—according to God's imperative—is almost addictive. It is the *only* wild ride I will purchase and stand in line for over and over again.

This chapter would not be complete without dissecting the word "reckless" and discussing what it means. Turns out the world has multiple translations. In the Hindi language, the adjective means "carefree, negligent, supine, and irresponsible." The Arabic translation includes "uninhibited, thoughtless, giddy, and flighty." Who says being carefree, uninhibited, or thoughtless is bad or inappropriate when it comes to helping others?

The original meaning of the Greek phrase "Beauty is in the eye of the beholder" is also relevant here. Just as we each view or perceive beauty differently, how we interpret and internalize certain words can be subjective too. While some might disagree, reckless giving, like beauty, can truly reside in the eye of the beholder.

Similarly, giddy, irresponsible, or flighty giving could mean sharing one's resources in a manner not limited by others' expectations. Consider an example of a single, middle-class parent's $5,000 annual charitable contribution to a nonprofit organization. While others might *assume* her donation is irresponsible and disproportionate to her income, she is much more compelled by knowing the monetary gift will feed thousands of children living in absolute poverty. Examples abound, and clearly how one "packages" her degree of giving is all about perspective.

When presented with the hopeless reality of others *and* the fact we have the means to help, God's call to action is clear. However, God also instructs us in Matthew 6:1 not to publicize our works: *"Watch out! Don't do your good deeds publicly, to be admired by others, for you will lose the reward from your Father in heaven."* Consider also Proverbs 27:2 in which we are admonished not to boast about any aspect of our lives: *"Let someone else praise you, not your own mouth—a stranger, not your own lips."*

As I drafted this book, I wrestled with the previous two verses because I wanted to be sure my motivation for talking about reckless giving did not fall in either category. I can say with a clear conscience that I only hope to release others from limiting thoughts about giving by sharing its potentially transformative impact on the giver, as well as everyone blessed to receive.

Will there be challenges? Yes. Will you sometimes question whether you should give? Absolutely. In fact, in Romans 7:19–20 Paul lamented, *"I want to do what is good, but I don't. I don't want to do what is wrong, but I do it anyway. But if I do what I don't want to do, I am not really the one doing wrong; it is sin living in me that does it."* When you have doubts, ask God to reveal to you whether underlying sins, such as judgmentalism, hatred, or chronic overspending, are contributing to your unwillingness to give as He commands.

Finally, I believe we should also dispel the notion, once and for all, that our earthly treasures will benefit us in any way when we die. 1 John 2:17 is just one of several sobering biblical reminders of our temporal riches and existence: *"And this world is fading away, along with everything that people crave. But anyone who does what pleases God will live forever."* Poet C.T. Studd also wisely said, "We have one life; it soon will be past; what we do for God is all that will last."[6]

CHAPTER 5:

ON THE RECEIVING END OF GIVING

The Philadelphia Eagles are by far my favorite professional football team. In fact, as I am a native Philadelphian, by default every professional sports team in the City of Brotherly Love is my favorite. That is, except the NBA Philadelphia 76ers, who jointly hold my loyalty with the Golden State Warriors team.

Because I laughingly feel compelled to justify my rationale about the 76ers, I'll explain it all boils down to history. You see, in the 1920s the *Philadelphia* Warriors franchise was based in Philadelphia. In 1963 the franchise was sold and then relocated to San Francisco, becoming the *San Francisco* Warriors. Although the newly formed 1963-era Philadelphia 76ers were transplants from the Syracuse Nationals team, to my uniquely logical way of thinking, today's Golden State Warriors are still akin to the 76ers. To some, that logic might sound like a twisted definition of loyalty, but it's my story and I am sticking to it!

Now, to all the avid football fans out there, you know the importance of every position on the team. The wide receiver's offensive priority is to catch the quarterback's passes. Once he makes the reception, only the defensive moves of the opposing team can prevent the wide receiver from scoring a touchdown. I think this description is also analogous to our giving.

When we pass the metaphorical football (gift) to people in need, like a quarterback's pass to the wide receiver, we not only give them a shot at scoring, but we also potentially eradicate the opposing tactics of their minds, the enemy (Satan), and other naysayers.

Case in point. I often share with people that as a child I grew up in relative poverty. I say "relative" poverty because while there was objective evidence of my family's financial lack, other aspects of my life were extraordinarily rich. Firstly, the kids in my West Philadelphia neighborhood played *hard*. Like Carole King wrote and James Taylor sang, *"Winter, spring, summer or fall, now all you got to do is call,"*[7] and we were out the front door, racing down the street, playing double Dutch or a boisterous game of tag. If I were a betting person, I would wager that I exercised more before the age of seventeen than I ever have as an adult. Now, I am not particularly proud of the starts and stops in my adult exercise routines, but hopefully you get my point.

I also remember playing outdoors in the winter months

and then tumbling through our front door soaking wet from the lavish amount of snow outside. Like my three siblings and neighborhood friends, I enjoyed the full-immersive experience—engaging in snowball fights, lying flat on my back and flailing my arms around to make snow angels, and eating snow as if it were an island delicacy.

Pausing to dry off, rest, and eat was an anti-climactic yet necessary evil. Back then, we had gray stand-alone metal gas radiators dispersed throughout our house. We would peel off our wet, soggy, snow-laden gloves, hats, and socks and lay them across the radiators to dry. On good days we sipped hot chocolate with marshmallows indoors as we waited for the next round of outdoor play.

It was not until I focused on the material things my friends had and compared them to my own that I noticed my family's financial condition. While others had store-bought clothes, my mother very skillfully sewed many of ours. Fortunately, my Dad was a career women's shoe salesman, so my sister and I never lacked footwear. I do not remember how my two brothers got their shoes, but I am pretty certain the majority were hand-me-downs. Talk about mug shots; we have pictures with us dressed in all kinds of color combinations and patterns. But we were always clothed.

The highlight of each week was Friday night when Daddy gave each of us a two-dollar allowance, and we usually each used it to buy a large bottle of our favorite soda. Pineapple was it for me, and I hoarded it just like my siblings guarded their favorite flavors. Although I cringe at the thought today, we loved sugary boxed cereal—the more sugar, the better. Depending on how we stretched our allowance, we each sometimes bought our favorite boxes of cereal too. Occasionally, our parents treated us to the most scrumptious hoagies from Mr. Ray's delicatessen on 55th & Pine Street. I couldn't get enough of the American cheese hoagies; they must have been loaded with at least one-half pound of cheese surrounded by the best Italian hoagie bread ever. So, while we lacked material things, the simple and abundant pleasures of food, fun, and family filled the gaps.

In 1976 when I was twelve years old, my parents separated, which made our financial situation worse. But 1976 was also the year that I accepted Jesus Christ as my personal Savior. Isn't it great how God works?

Initially, my mother secured an apartment on South 56th Street, right around the corner from my childhood home on 55th & Addison Street. I recall sharing a bedroom with my sister on the first floor, at the front of the apartment, while my two brothers shared a bunk bed in the basement. My mother repurposed a room next to the kitchen for her bedroom. As you might guess, that location did not give her much privacy as we frequently passed through her area to get to the kitchen or go out the back door.

Ms. Henry, our landlord, was a godsend and a reckless

giver too. She was a Black single parent of two sons and a daughter with multiple disabilities. In the 1970s those socioeconomic challenges were enough without having to deal with tenants like my mom who could not always make timely rent payments. While I loved my father dearly, his sporadic child support payments, in such meager amounts as determined by the court system, meant my mom had to work three part-time jobs as a school crossing guard, Avon representative, and Tupperware dealer. If it were not for Ms. Henry and other people like our church pastor, we would certainly have missed many meals.

I also remember our mother always seemed to have more coins than dollars in her purse. While my siblings and I received either free or reduced school lunches, oftentimes we would still ask Mommy for extra money to get snacks. I still cannot shake the memory of taking her change and knowingly leaving her next to nothing in her purse. Unfortunately, at that age it was all about what I wanted or needed at the time. That is why Mommy can ask me to do almost anything for her today. If I can afford it, I have the time, and it is legal, she can have it!

About one year after we moved into that apartment, my dad moved out of our family home, and we moved back in. While we were optimistic at first, the financial struggles got even worse.

There were times when the utility companies turned off our water, gas, or electric service for late- or non-payment.

The water service cutoff was the most embarrassing because the oversized water company truck would drive down the street, stop, and then open the valve or manhole closest to our home. Everyone on the street could see what was happening. We drank and cooked with water our neighbors gave us and took birdbaths either in our house or theirs. Back then, bottled water was not available, so we couldn't even store up water for those inevitable metaphorical rainy days.

I also remember coming home on a particularly chilly night after the city suspended our gas service. The house was so cold that I saw my breath form like a puff of smoke every time I spoke or exhaled. Fortunately, we had plenty of blankets and we shared beds for warmth when necessary. Whenever the electric service was suspended, preserving food in the refrigerator was a greater priority than being able to see objects around the house. Plus, our house was directly across from a streetlight, so I do not recall ever experiencing a pitch-black night.

What I remember most vividly about our financial condition was my mother sending me to the corner grocery store to ask for food on credit. Now, I was raised not to talk back to my parents, surrogate or biological aunts and uncles, teachers, or any other adult. So, when Mommy told me to go, I did it without questioning her or complaining. The walks to the corner store took forever, as I looked around occasionally to see if anyone was watching me. Although the store was only half a block away, I dreaded facing Mr.

Smith and his son Mr. John once again, so I dragged my feet as a means to delay my inevitable embarrassment.

    I still recall the grocery store owners' looks of pity and resignation as they reluctantly took our order on credit and then handed me the food. It was reckless giving on their part for sure because of the low probability that it would be the last time, never mind my mother being able to pay the new bill on time—if ever. I honestly do not remember how often my three siblings had to do the same thing, but I am sure they had similar experiences. I also think back at where we were as a nation; I was born in 1964, the year the Civil Rights Act passed. While we lived in the North, the early to mid-70s was still a time heavily marred by racism and poverty amongst Black families as we fought for our self-esteem too. My sister recalls her school bus being stoned and people hurling racial epithets at the Black students aboard. In hindsight I am even more thankful to those grocery store owners—who I think were Jewish—as they helped us, and probably others in our neighborhood, with our basic needs for food and employment. Years later as adults, my siblings and I talked about finding the store owners and repaying them with interest, but unfortunately, that opportunity never materialized. Even today I wish we could simply say "thank you" to them or any of their surviving family members because their generosity made such a huge difference in our lives.

    During my senior year of high school, I applied to several colleges and universities. I was accepted to three:

Fisk University, Oberlin College, and the U.S. Military Academy Preparatory School. While the prospect of leaving home was exciting, when it came down to it, my family obviously could not afford the tuition, and I did not have other support to help me navigate the financial aid process. Although I was guaranteed a free ride at the military academy, at that age I could not fathom "giving away" twelve years of my life—four years of college plus up to eight years of obligated military service afterward. Instead, I went straight into the Army at the age of seventeen.

In case I still have not adequately described the correlation between an unforgettable element of my childhood and the game of football, let me try another approach.

While experiencing childhood poverty, I did not know those experiences were necessary for me to learn humility and *feel* lack, that they would produce in me a burning desire to help others, or that poverty was only relative to my physical surroundings and belongings—not necessarily a reflection of my state of mind and spirit. As a child, I was unknowingly building up an empathy for others that would later convert to my spiritual gift of giving. God knew back then the plans He had for me.

To this day I am convinced that God gave Ms. Henry, Mr. Smith, Mr. John, our pastor, and many others the hearts to serve which, in turn, gave me (and my siblings) a shot at scoring in life. I could have been that child not raised by the proverbial village, or someone bombarded with struggles that left me feeling dejected or unworthy. Instead, God granted me those childhood experiences to instill compassion, humility, lovingkindness, and generosity within my imperfect self. So, when I hear about a mother struggling to raise her kids, a local food drive, or the needs of an organization that supports those living in poverty, I do not have to over-analyze the situation or pray about whether to help. Instead, I feel compelled to respond with empathy first, followed quickly by an offer to help. My past lack was extremely purposeful in that it predisposed me to give recklessly in my future. I hear King Solomon's voice in Proverbs 28:27 loud and clear: *"Whoever gives to the poor will lack nothing, but those who close their eyes to poverty will be cursed."*

As a very important aside as I begin to close out this chapter, I want to also expound on the value of relationships during this spiritually formative time of my life. As a child, I was blessed to know several special people who carried me through those tough times. Two people who readily come to mind, and we still talk regularly, are Carla Elam and Eugene Mills (whom we call Gene). A third person is Laura Hawkins.

Carla was undoubtedly my first best friend. She lived down the street and still has the cutest, deepest dimples and a smile that travels directly to her eyes. She also wore two pigtails a lot; that is, until another girl "accidentally" cut off one of them while we were sitting on Carla's front steps one day. One of the most beautiful things about our earlier relationship was my special connection not only with her but also with her mom. I would hang out at their house for hours and hours, listening to old-school music and soaking in the wisdom her mom spoke. When I hear the phrase "It takes a village to raise a child," Carla's mom is one of the people who immediately comes to mind. I am so blessed to still have a relationship with them both, plus one of Carla's brothers.

My good friend Gene's birthday is on February 28, whereas mine is on February 29—Leap Day during a Leap Year. He is a few years older than me, but every year to this day we get excited about our birthdays. When it is not a Leap Year, we both celebrate on February 28. I have always thought of Gene as family. Like a brother, he looked out for and encouraged me, and he was a big part of my youthful passion for running. Our bond extends to our connections with each other's moms, our mutual love of music, and our steadfast commitments to Christ. When we make the time, we talk about big and small things. I am so grateful for the gift of our longstanding friendship.

Laura was our next-door neighbor. While Gene was more like an older brother, Laura was more like a younger mother. I cannot adequately describe the solace I got from going to her house to talk and unwind amidst the financial and emotional complexities of my childhood. Many days I would go to her house for a meal, to dance and laugh, or to have a deep conversation. Her mother, now deceased, also really helped us, but my deeper relationship was with Laura. While I have thought about her profuse kindness many times over the years, I do not think I have ever adequately thanked Laura for being a sounding board, particularly in my teenage years, and for her gift of really caring about me. Hopefully, I have rectified that oversight through these words.

Before I finally close this chapter, I have a question and challenge for you. As you look back over your own life, do you recall painful periods of lack that later manifested as periods of abundance? That lack may or may not have been monetary; perhaps you experienced it through personal relationships, communications, feeling unsupported, or feeling like you did not belong. If so, I challenge you to consider the possibility that God allowed those dark times so that later in your life you would be passionate about serving others in those very same areas—finances, relationships, communication, support, or belongingness— without worldly restraint or reservation. Here are a few biblical passages and a quote that validate your call to action:

> *"If someone has enough money to live well and sees a brother or sister in need but shows no compassion—how can God's love be in that person?" (1 John 3:17)*

> *"Do not withhold good from those who deserve it when it's in your power to help them." (Proverbs 3:27)*

"Give to those who ask, and don't turn away from those who want to borrow." (Matthew 5:42)

"The purpose of life is not to be happy. It is to be useful, to be honorable, to be compassionate, to have it make some difference that you have lived and lived well."

— **Ralph Waldo Emerson**

CHAPTER 6:

BY DESIGN OR COINCIDENCE?

———•⟨⟩•———

Have you ever noticed when you are introduced to something or someone new or different, suddenly you start seeing that thing or person all the time? A new couple at church, cars the same make or model as the one you just purchased ... the list goes on. This phenomenon has happened to me too many times to doubt its validity.

After joining the military at the age of seventeen, I relocated to ten geographic regions over the next thirty-nine years. On average I moved every four years between 1982 and 2021. After my initial military assignment at Fort Jackson, South Carolina, for basic and advanced training, I relocated to Fort Hood, Texas, for my first permanent duty station. After David and I met and married in Texas, we moved to Fort Belvoir, Virginia, which is also where I received an honorable discharge. From there we moved due to David's military reassignments to Frankfurt, Germany; Minneapolis, Minnesota; Fort Monmouth, New Jersey; and Macon, Georgia. Post-military service we did either partial or wholesale moves to Powder Springs, Georgia; Fairfax, Manassas, and Sterling, Virginia; and finally Douglasville, Georgia, which we now call home. That does not even account for two interim moves my kids and I made to Philadelphia, Pennsylvania, as we awaited military orders to join David.

One very noticeable common thread with each move was the time it took me to memorize new driving routes. With the introduction of global positioning software, I initially relied on a cell phone map application to get me from point A to point B until I became familiar with a new area. Inexplicably, once I learned a route, I began noticing houses or landmarks that I had not seen when I was becoming acclimated to the area. In the learning process, I essentially developed tunnel vision for anything else around me because my focus was only on the most direct approach to reach any given destination.

I have also noticed that I am more observant of my surroundings when I shift to being a passenger rather than the driver on what I believe to be a familiar route. When I leave the driver's seat, I am more aware of what is around me and enjoy the scenery that I had not noticed before.

So what is my point? I compare my driver and passenger experiences to the heightened awareness I have of people who are, or appear to be, homeless. Like a human magnet, I believe the Holy Spirit puts me in the metaphorical passenger seat, even while I am driving, and

He intentionally draws me to certain people to help them according to His will. And yes, while driving I have made U-turns or pulled off the road (nothing dangerous or illegal, I assure you!) because I saw, and was drawn to, someone in need. Thank God for the assurances we find in 1 Peter 3:13–14: *"Now, who will want to harm you if you are eager to do good? But even if you suffer for doing what is right, God will reward you for it. So don't worry or be afraid of their threats."*

Unfortunately, many believe that people who are experiencing homelessness did something wrong that led to their deprived condition or circumstances. On more occasions than I care to remember, unsympathetic and uninformed people have said "they" are either drunkards or drug addicts who have blown a good thing to feed their habits. How unfair given many people, like my mom when I was growing up, must make tough choices between paying for food, medication, or rent. Then there are those who do not earn sufficient wages despite the number of hours they work and therefore find themselves in less-than-ideal living conditions. Let's not forget socioeconomic disparities and institutionalized racist practices that are, sadly, still alive and rampant. The scenarios abound and can be as unique as human fingerprints.

While it is not my intent to boast about those I have helped, each of the three recent situations I encountered reminds me of the small things we can do when we see our brothers and sisters in need and have the means to help.

GIVING, RECKLESSLY

I did not bring an ultimate solution, but hopefully those encounters brought temporary relief and showed them they were noticed. Perhaps coincidentally, all of these people were men, they reminded me of my father as he aged, and two of the three popped into my view while I was driving. I'll use fictitious names, although in each instance they told me their real names:

I met Robert in Myrtle Beach, South Carolina, while my husband and I were vacationing. While driving, I noticed a man who could barely walk as he carried an overstuffed backpack, a duffel bag, and several other disposable bags. I circled in my car and slowly pulled into the parking lot where he was walking. I inched closer, rolled down my window, and asked him whether he would accept some money to buy a meal. I also had a bag of items that I kept in the car and passed on to Robert, but he struggled to grab anything more. We struck up a conversation, and he noticed a cord was dangling outside my closed passenger-side door. He asked politely whether it was alright to open the door to free what turned out to be my cell phone charger cord, and I told him yes. It was apparent that he and I were both exercising extreme caution, and I could sense that he was a good man.

After putting the cord on my seat, firmly shutting the door, and stepping back, Robert briefly shared that he was in a tough place—trying to work through some spiritual issues in his life. Like so many others who are alone and homeless, I could tell he craved conversation with someone who would listen and just acknowledge his existence. When he finally walked away, I grieved for his condition and asked God to free him from distress and give him more provisions soon.

    For a 2023 Christmas present, my son gave me two tickets to a popular musical show in Atlanta. I intentionally arrived early, parked my car, and began walking around to re-familiarize myself with the area until my friend arrived. It was cold, so I decided to find a Starbucks café for a hot cup of coffee. As I approached the street I needed to cross, out of the corner of my eye I saw a man, and the Holy Spirit instantly drew me to him. The older gentleman had on a dirty, bulky coat and was wearing hospital attire with Crocs as footwear. For anyone who does not know, Crocs are thick plastic clog-like sandals with holes across the main part of the shoe. It looked like he was also wearing a thin pair of socks. As I cautiously walked up beside him, to get his attention, I lightly but firmly asked his name and where he was going. He kept up his tippy-toe-like pace while partially turning to face me as he pointed to a nearby commercial building where he said the tenants had previously let him come inside to warm up. After a few more steps, he tugged on the gray metal handle of the glass door but realized this time the entrance was closed. Jumping at the opportunity, I asked whether he would like to go get coffee with me at Starbucks and whether he could walk that far. He nodded happily, we crossed a narrow two-way street, and then we walked inside.

Now, I am not a frequent Starbucks patron, so I was really glad I had an unused $15 gift card from Christmas to spend on this man (Howard) at a minimum. He studied the menu for a few seconds and then asked for something sweet, so I ordered him a breakfast sandwich, lemon cake, and lemonade. Even in the bitter cold weather, I found it very funny that Howard craved sweets more than a hot drink, which reminded me so much of my dad and his sweet tooth. Understanding that we all like special things in our food, when Howard inquired, I asked the cashier whether they had ketchup he could put on his sandwich. They did not, but we got Agave nectar as a substitute for the syrup he wanted. At some point I remembered that I had a bulky gray blanket and more bags of items in my car. By then Howard had started to eat, and I prayed that no one would give us a hard time about him sitting in the main dining area close to the cash register. Sadly, several people looked at him somewhat disapprovingly, and I doggedly stared back. Howard agreed to wait there until I came back, and I was happy that he was still warm and eating when I returned. I placed the bagged blanket and other items on the floor close to him. It was time for me to go, and I briefly prayed that God would provide him more soon.

Steve crossed through a vacant lot, barely holding on to the bags he carried. I was driving home, and his movements in my left peripheral view got my attention. Honestly, my first inclination was to continue driving because of a task I had waiting at home, but the picture of him locked itself in my mind, and I couldn't shake it. About a block away now, I made a legal, safe U-turn and eventually pulled up near him in an old gas station. It was daytime, and I quickly checked my surroundings before getting out of my car and calling out to him. Thankfully, just that morning I had put another medium-sized clean blanket in my trunk, so I emptied a large plastic tote bag to hold the blanket and his belongings. I also had two small bags of items that I usually carry for times like these. One of the first things I noticed was Steve's curled, excessively dry, and wrinkled fingers. I offered and he gladly accepted my "good" winter gloves. I called them my good gloves because I have a secondary systemic condition called Raynaud's phenomena and those gloves kept my hands warm. After a slight mutual hesitation, Steve also allowed me to put a mock scarf around his neck to help block the cold. We talked a little bit, and he tried to assure me that he was close to his final destination. As I drove away, I looked over at him on the sidewalk, and our eyes briefly connected. With a little more confidence, he hoisted his new tote bag over his shoulder and continued walking. As always, I silently prayed that God would provide him with more soon.

As I think back on my humbling experiences with these three men, I know God did not want me to overthink or analyze their needs. Frankly, how people became disadvantaged is not my business—a concern, yes, but not to the extent that I should pass judgment and conclude they do not need assistance. Be forewarned. Each of us either has reached or might reach a fork in the road where an unexpected calamity, job loss, or other circumstance outside of our control can have a detrimental impact on our ability to secure food and affordable housing.

Speaking of passing judgment, have you ever heard the biblical story of the adulterous woman?

We find in John 8:3–7 that the Pharisees brought an adulterous woman to Jesus and sought His perspective on whether the woman should be stoned to death. Their ulterior motive was to test Jesus to bring up charges against Him. Imagine the Pharisees' remorse and embarrassment when Jesus flipped the proverbial script by saying in verse 7: *"All right, but let the one who has never sinned throw the first stone!"* So, whether it be an addiction, bad habit, poor decision, or intentional wrongdoing, this Scriptural imperative disqualifies us from any self-righteous, hypocritical tendency to judge others because we would all fail that test.

Along those same lines, one of my all-time favorite phrases is "fundamental attribution error." While you can certainly look up its formal definition, this phrase describes our human tendency to pre-judge and make inferences about someone else's behavior while underestimating the effect of external factors on any given situation. For example, if you see a woman walking on a busy road, does that mean she is homeless or does not have a car? Is it possible she chose to walk on the busy road for exercise, or that she simply does not prefer driving? I'll give you a real-life example. After I moved to Georgia, I met Henrietta Hardnett (now Smith). We attended the same church and became good friends. At some point we became walking partners, and one way we would break up the monotony was doing what I dubbed "destination walking." Many days we would walk up and down a major highway with sidewalks in Marietta, Georgia, and if we needed to pick up a few items at the grocery store or a retail store along the way, we set our sights on that destination. Now to someone driving along the same highway, we might have looked like people who needed a ride, but that was far from the truth. However, if we or the woman in my first example were homeless and did not have cars, is it right to assume we had committed some grievous act or crime, so we are now paying for our transgressions? Unfortunately, the variety of circumstances and frequency with which we make fundamental attribution errors are endless, but God's Word never wavers: *"Do not judge others, and you will not be judged."* (Matthew 7:1).

So, you might be thinking, what about those people who do take advantage of others' desire to give recklessly? Frankly, those possibilities do not bother me at all because my imperfect self gets to make mistakes! If I do err when giving to others, that alternative is infinitely preferable to passing judgment about them or their circumstances. I would rather still give with the intent to demonstrate authentic love, empathy, and compassion. If someone intends to connive or deceive me, I find peace in God's Word found in

Galatians 6:7, which says, *"Don't be misled—you cannot mock the justice of God. You will always harvest what you plant."* Ultimately, my failure to act when I have the means to help contradicts God's unwavering instruction—and He *will* have the final say.

Now, please do not get me wrong. I can spot a con game too. I have observed "teams" of people holding up signs at busy intersections and adults using their children to gain the sympathy of passersby. I have firsthand experience with people who "borrowed" money from me with no intention of ever paying me back. I also know that helping sometimes actually hurts people who continue to make poor choices after being presented with better options. For these reasons, I am thankful for the discernment God gave me along with my spiritual gift of giving. I also pray that my gift always aligns with this imperative and warning:

> *Share each other's burdens, and in this way obey the law of Christ. If you think you are too important to help someone, you are only fooling yourself. You are not that important. Pay careful attention to your own work, for then you will get the satisfaction of a job well done, and you won't need to compare yourself to anyone else. For we are each responsible for our own conduct. (Galatians 6:2–5)*

By design or coincidence—who knows? What I *am* sure of is that we can transform our minds and hearts when we open them to the possibility that either scenario is possible, and each presents us with an opportunity to truly see and help those in need.

CHAPTER 7:

WHEN THE BLESSINGS OVERRIDE THE PROGNOSIS

Each day, I wake up with a stream of thoughts—what is on my to-do list, what I did not accomplish from yesterday's to-do list, and why either list is even important in the scheme of things. The latter thought inevitably gets the least recognition or credit as the other two dominate and virtually guarantee a day of endless activities. As I roll out of bed, most of the time with some degree of pain and using a chiropractor-prescribed technique, I subconsciously push aside the physical impediments that threaten to hinder the day's agenda. The truth is, if I were to consciously defer to my "normal" pain and the medical diagnosis that I received over thirty-three years ago, there would be many days when I would be inclined to do nothing. Oh, but the story I am about to share with you is one of victory, mercy, healing, and an emphatic declaration that only God has the final say.

When I was diagnosed with systemic lupus

erythematosus, or SLE, in 1991, I did not know the diagnosis would eventually moderate my physical abilities and regulate how I would react to stress in positive and negative ways. I also did not know that I would eventually be able to encourage others suffering from this chronic autoimmune disease, or how closely Charles Dickens's famous quote "It was the best of times, it was the worst of times …"[8] aligns with the ebbs and flows of lupus. At this point, I ask for your patience as I recap key periods and events in my life surrounding this cruel disease, as well as God's never-ending mercy that continues to override the prognosis.

While serving in the Army, I began experiencing a seemingly unrelated array of physical and systemic signs and symptoms. This mystery began unfolding in the late summer of 1982 while I was stationed at Fort Hood, Texas (since renamed Fort Cavazos). I still vividly recall lying in the twin bed in my barracks room, shivering feverishly although I had turned off the air conditioning unit and covered myself with a heavy Army olive drab green wool blanket. The weather in central Texas was extremely hot that year; we heard stories about cows dying on farms and dire warnings not to leave children unattended in cars. Eventually, I summoned up enough energy to go to the installation military hospital where I was initially diagnosed with dehydration and pyelonephritis, or kidney inflammation. I vividly recall my pain and trauma as the nurses searched for good veins in my arms to start an intravenous infusion. They tapped and prodded with their fingers and gingerly inserted sharp needles over and over until finally finding a spot that would accommodate a catheter to gradually re-hydrate my body. It was a horrible and frightening experience.

Fast forward to 1986. During an outdoor military exercise in Virginia, I could not understand or explain to others why my fingertips and toes throbbed so painfully and lacked color. I remember feeling so uncharacteristically despondent during that outdoor exercise that I risked disciplinary action by telling my company leaders that I was going inside our tent to get warm no matter what they commanded. From a pain perspective, I also recall going to my first appointment at a large well-known Army medical center and slithering desperately along the walls as I tried to make it to different places in the facility. I later learned that massive inflammation had set in, which was also indicative of an acute serious condition. These two occasions marked the beginning of a long journey toward discovering what was going on in my body.

Thankfully during these years, I was blessed to give birth to my two eldest children, Demetrius and Tiffany, in 1983 and 1986, respectively. By the end of 1987, I received an honorable discharge as well as a documented diagnosis of rheumatoid arthritis.

I characterize 1989–1991 as my initial period of lupus enlightenment. This time was marred by confusion and uncertainty as my body demanded immediate specialized medical attention. It was during an accompanied tour with my husband in Frankfurt, Germany, that I began experiencing widespread joint and muscle pain that at times limited my ability to walk even a few steps. Based on protocol, I was enrolled in the military's exceptional family member program and recommended for immediate medical care when we returned to the United States. Most memorable was my confusion, as a doctor at the Philadelphia Naval Hospital clinic eventually told me in August 1991 that I had lupus. It was a medical term I did not even know existed, never mind the potential magnitude of the disease. Confused, I asked the doctor to repeat himself and then tell me what it meant. My future medical care team would later qualify my condition as lupus nephritis, characterized by chronic kidney disease. However, this new turn in the road, while painful and frightening, would prove to be yet another example of God's perpetual benevolence.

My husband comes from a large family. So in late 1992 when I learned I was pregnant again, I was so excited and thought the perfect Christmas gift for him that year would be news of our third expected child. I was so sure he would be ecstatic too that I decided to put a copy of the ultrasound pregnancy test results in a Christmas card as his only gift. Imagine my disbelief, shock, and grief when I learned soon after the good news that I had miscarried—not in a traumatic or lingering fashion—but quietly. The only explanation my medical care team in Minnesota gave me was the miscarriage was caused by either the disease or the side effects of my prescribed medication, Plaquenil. So, instead of the Christmas gift I planned for my husband that year, I delivered the sad news of my miscarriage.

God's divine benevolence showed up yet again, though! Not long after the miscarriage, I conceived again. It was a pretty normal pregnancy, and in November 1993 our third child, Kiana, was born. But the blessings did not stop there. Over the years I was still pursuing my undergraduate degree, taking classes whenever and wherever I could. In March 1994, four months after Kiana's birth and almost thirteen years after my high school graduation, I finally received my bachelor's degree in business administration. This accomplishment alone is a testament to God's favor and His ability to order our steps amidst the most challenging times and situations.

In 1996 our fourth child, Mikhala, was born in New Jersey. This pregnancy was noticeably different, though. Because of my lupus diagnosis, my obstetric care team carefully monitored, planned, and executed every aspect of my pregnancy. Unlike with my other pregnancies, my doctor scheduled Mikhala's delivery, and I felt confident and trustful of the medical care I received.

While I dubbed 1989–1991 as my initial period of lupus enlightenment, I thought I was in a fairly stable, controlled state between 1992–2000 except for the miscarriage in late 1992. I visited my doctors regularly; faithfully took the prescription steroid, Prednisone, and Plaquenil; and had blood and urine lab tests done routinely.

The lupus flare-up and resulting challenges I experienced from 2001–2002 surprised and fully awakened me to the serious complications associated with the disease. In those two years, I learned the value of having a personal understanding of my condition; the importance of having qualified, sincere, and proactive physicians; and the difference effective and timely medical treatments can make in the longevity of one's life. Facetiously speaking, during this period I had the dubious "honor" of developing Stage 4 kidney disease (Stage 5 is considered end-stage), which my rheumatologist and nephrologist arrested through chemotherapy, higher doses of Prednisone, and aggressive follow-up treatment. What I still cannot understand or explain is how the disease progressed so acutely when I had been very intentional about keeping follow-up medical appointments and taking the recommended recurring battery of laboratory tests leading up to that crisis. Unfortunately, what I do believe is racial and socioeconomic medical treatment disparities still exist—whether intentional or unintentional. I will not digress further except to say that God was still looking out for me in His divine, incomparable, and benevolent way.

From an extended crisis perspective, no other noteworthy events have occurred since my kidney scare in 2002 that underscored the seriousness of lupus and its effects on my life. Like most lupus sufferers, I learned my lessons the hard way, as they say, and those lessons shaped how I live today. Thankfully, my lupus journey now primarily consists of remissions, with the occasional mystical "rule out" and flare-up managed through recurring doctor visits, maintenance prescriptions, and on-demand medical treatments and hospitalizations.

As I end this chapter, I would be remiss in not reiterating the lessons I learned along the way, which include the following:

- *Knowing the disease*
- *Demanding the best from your physicians*
- *Refusing to accept unqualified information or foregone conclusions*
- *Living each day to the fullest*

Most importantly, as I reflect on God's extreme benevolence, I would be grossly remiss if I did not acknowledge His continuous presence and faithfulness through it all. Not a day passes that I am not reminded of God's sovereignty, power to heal, and unmerited mercy. He allowed trials and challenges that gave me a testimony that encourages and comforts others as they navigate the uncertainties of lupus.

CHAPTER 8:

THE BLESSING OF HAVING RESILIENT CHILDREN

My husband and I are so grateful to our four children for their unknowing generosity too. They, like many other military children, collectively experienced so many moves, separations, and other adjustments primarily during David's military career. Each time we moved, they had to start at new schools and churches, find new friends, and acclimate to a new physical environment. Their bedrooms looked different. Their doctors, teachers, and classmates changed. They had to let go of warm relationships and, for a time, recreational sports and arts they loved. While we visited our respective extended families in Philadelphia, Pennsylvania, and Valdosta, Georgia, as much as possible, our children missed out on cultivating close relationships with their grandparents, aunts, uncles, and cousins who lived there.

I am so grateful for the God-wink blessings of their

resilience, tenacity, and ability to adapt in the midst of it all. Today, those blessings show up in the creative, adventurous, and generous adults they have become. In birth order, here are their accounts of the gifts they unknowingly gave us—and their challenges—while growing up as military dependents. By the way, part of my three daughters' accounts refer to a time when I took a job away from them, at the same time David was deployed overseas. You will hear the whole story when I tell you about my friend Roxie in chapter 11.

Demetrius Nelson

Being a military "brat" had its benefits and boulders. The benefit of it was that I got to explore different parts of the world, primarily different States that I probably would never have had enough courage to move to as an adult because of that kind of conditioning. I adopted different mindsets based on the local culture, and in some parts, it was essential for the development of my personality. When people ask me where I'm from, I often tell them that I'm from Jersey. I was there throughout middle school and half of high school. In my extensive experience as a classroom teacher, I know children's personalities are mainly developed between middle and high school. So, if you are a Northerner, especially if you are from New York, New Jersey, or the Philadelphia area, we talk, walk, and think differently. In my experience, those who are from the South understand me more when they find out I primarily grew up in the North. So the strength of my opinion on certain matters and issues stems from living in resilient environments up North.

The boulders would be that I have always been envious of my friends who were born and raised in cities where I felt like a temporary visitor by way of my dad's military assignments. As an adult, my recollection of friends is limited to where my dad was stationed. When my dad was reassigned, I couldn't afford to maintain communication with all of them because cell phones didn't exist and our parents weren't allowing us to run up their landline phone bills to talk with my best friends in Minnesota and New Jersey. Instead, I had to wait for my parents to call their friends who were also the parents of my best friends. It's rare today to see those types of relationships. As an adult, I've been fortunate to have adult relationships with my best friends from elementary and high school because we all understand how life happens, interrupts, and sometimes thwarts our plans to keep in touch when we move away or attend college. Now, do I wish that I were born and raised in one place? Yes, but I realize that who I am is not just for me, but more so for the benefit of others in the society that I live in. My past produced my personality, which empowered me so I can produce good works that educate, enlighten, and empower others. So it rings true when it says in Romans 8:28 that all things work together for the good of those who love God and are called according to His purpose. Believing and operating in this truth without restraint is my gift to the world.

Tiffany Alexander

Regarding my experience as a military child, overall I have mixed feelings about it. I did not like the fact that we had to move every four years, make new friends, go to new schools, and adapt to new environments, or that those relationships sometimes did not continue. On the other hand, I did like seeing other States and cities and people. It got a little tougher as I got older, but the only time that I took exception to our life was when we moved from New Jersey to Georgia. I left my best friend in NJ, and we both had a hard time with that. I remember having my own trail of tears as we took the long drive *down South. Going into middle school in the eighth grade was hard too, not only as a new student but also as someone from the North. We quickly learned that there is this North-South dynamic in terms of how you speak and how you act and things of that sort, so, you know, the kids in my new school would pick on me and tease me.*

But I will say that moving to Georgia was the first time that I knew or remembered that I actually cared about my grades. I don't know what made that happen—maybe because I noticed the grading systems were more relaxed in Georgia than in New Jersey. Perhaps that helped me too, but I also just became more serious about my education.

When we lived in Warner Robins while Dad was deployed in Iraq, and we stayed with our grandmother while our mom worked in Kennesaw, I only remember that being my senior year of high school. I had the choice of being able to stay in the same school where I had developed great friendships—one of which I still have to this day—so I was fine with that choice. I also remember having a good time in my senior year. I missed my mother, but I don't think I missed her as much as maybe my two younger sisters did. From what I recall, I was just in a lot of extracurricular activities that kept me busy. It was always nice to see my mom when she came home, and I don't think I necessarily liked that she turned around so quickly, but I understood that she had to because of her new job.

I was aware of the living arrangement my mom had with Ms. Roxie; I thought that was nice of Ms. Roxie, and I didn't have any concerns about my mom staying with her. I do remember taking the call when she was offered that job; in fact, I was happy about it because I wanted to leave Warner Robins soon after graduation. Her new job was my "get out of jail free card" outside of planning to attend Spelman College in Atlanta. I just knew that opportunity brought me one step closer.

Kiana Nelson

I avoided writing this because it's not all fun memories for me. I have abandonment issues that carried over into my adulthood. I lost my best friend the same year my dad was deployed due to the 9/11 terrorist attack on the Twin Towers. I was always waiting for the call that something happened to him, and that's an anxiety no kid—no person—should ever have to experience. It got worse when my mom accepted a new job in another city, and she was commuting and also living with a coworker. I still remember the limo coming to pick her up, lol. It felt like the SpongeBob episode where everyone is looking out the window at everyone else having fun.

At some point, I felt it was noble and necessary for me to follow in my dad's footsteps, but there was no clear line of success that would encompass my skills. I even scored high on the Armed Services Vocational Aptitude Battery, or ASVAB test. In another world, I could see myself in the CIA since I like the thrill of action shows. But because of my experience as a military dependent, I would never again subject myself or any kids I have to the life of a military family.

I used to feel so happy hearing the national anthem and thanking service members in uniform. But there was a point in the fifth grade when I stopped standing up for the pledge of allegiance. Even at that age, I saw how people of different religions were treated, and racism was even more evident. My teachers tried to discipline me for not standing for the pledge, but telling them I was a military kid helped justify my position. I know we would not have our present quality of life had it not been for the military, but I do wish my childhood had been different.

Mikhala Nelson

I was fortunate enough to not have to endure as many moves at the hands of the military as my older siblings did. A few years after I was born (and earlier than I can remember), our final military move was from my birthplace in New Jersey to the mid-sized town of Warner Robins, Georgia, which is about two hours south of Atlanta. Some of my earliest memories there were from my time at Westside Elementary, where I had a best friend named Doreen. We were thick as thieves and remained friends as long as I can remember the four years we lived here. I remember my mom working tirelessly at her writing business, called Just Write for You, while she attended graduate school. Then my mom got the opportunity of a lifetime to take a job at a non-profit agency in metro Atlanta. Before I could process what was happening, we were relocating again—this time to Powder Springs, Georgia, a place that I now largely consider to be my hometown.

While I do remember being upset at the idea of changing schools and no longer being

> *friends with people like Doreen, I had no trouble establishing new friendships in the school I transferred to in Powder Springs. In fact, my best friend of now twenty years was in my second-grade class, and we've been inseparable since the day I was the new girl in class. In hindsight, I'm incredibly grateful that my parents' paths brought me to Powder Springs. My fondest memories happened in that very town, and the friendships I formed—that I still hold in adulthood—are irreplaceable and wouldn't have happened without my parents' lives taking this form.*
>
> *If you ask my siblings, they have had some more difficult feelings to process as a result of the frequent moves, and those changes might have had more of an impact on their childhoods. But for me, I consider it formative in my upbringing, and I wouldn't have had it any other way!*

As I read and pondered what our now-adult children shared with me about their experiences as military dependents, things they never or rarely expressed while they were growing up, I am reminded of the significance of choices parents make every day. I think about God's command to us in Proverbs 22:6, which says, *"Direct your children onto the right path, and when they are older, they will not leave it."* Amid their oftentimes unsettling experiences, I truly hope each of our four children received the gift of knowing which way to go.

From left to right: Tiffany, Kiana, Leslie (me), David, Mikhala, and Demetrius at my 60th birthday party in 2024.

CHAPTER 9:

WHEN SAYING "NO" IS BENEFICIAL

I am a strong believer that there is nothing new under the sun. While the details, places, or people might change, other aspects of human interactions generally never do—*like the inability to just say "No" when we really should, and we mean it.* Know that I count myself squarely in that number; however, I want to do better, starting today.

We have three basic options when someone asks us to do something, to be someplace, or to make a commitment. We can say "Yes," "No," or "Maybe." Some people qualify their answers by saying, "Yes, if my husband agrees." Or, "No, unless you select another restaurant that does not serve seafood." Arguably, "Maybe" is the clearest response in these two examples, but at least the respondent has informed the other person of some contingency that, once worked out, should quickly lead to a definitive answer.

It gets more complicated when a relative, friend, or significant other needs a favor—let's just say to borrow money until the next payday. Instead of saying "No" because we do not have the extra cash, or we do not trust the person will pay us back, one might hedge by saying, "I have to ask my wife first." Now that example can be a bit comical or downright dishonest, especially when the person is not inclined to ask his wife's opinion or permission for anything else related to finances!

When it comes to our actual or potential business relationships, the stakes might get a little higher. Consider the sales executive who invests many hours preparing and then pulls off a stellar presentation. The potential client promises to follow up "soon," even though he knows the price of the new service or product is not within the company's budget. Then there is the manager who has the authority to promote, but when asked about a timeline, she consistently tells an employee, "Maybe next year" without further explanation. Notice that I described the latter person as a manager, not a leader.

Similarly, if we do not have the bandwidth to accept another volunteer position, it would be best to let the organization know right away so they can find someone else to fill the need. As my final example, consider the candidate for a new salaried position who might forego accepting a different position because the hiring manager chose to leave the candidate in limbo by saying "We'll get back to you soon" instead of a categoric "No." But I do understand that human resources practices might limit what can be conveyed to candidates during interviews.

So here's my point. We are all given the same twenty-four hours each day, seven days a week. Many of us plan and prioritize what we will do in that time, and there are often opportunity costs associated with our day-to-day decisions.

When we know that we cannot or do not want to take a certain action, the fair thing to do is just say so. As with the biblical Golden Rule ("Do unto others as you would have them do unto you"), we should respect the priorities and limited resources of others even when those things do not align with our priorities and resources. This respect should then compel us to become more honest at the moment, and more comfortable just saying "No" when that answer is a true indicator of our limitations and that is what we mean.

Finally, consider these four truths whenever you are conflicted about giving materially or giving more of yourself to others:

1. We all need sacred, physical, and mental rest.

2. The airplane oxygen mask analogy: To survive, you must put on your oxygen mask first before helping anyone else.

3. You simply cannot help everyone, everywhere, every time. Establish an appropriate giving-life balance.

4. Helping hurts others when your actions are enabling, insensitive, un-informed, or undertaken with ulterior motives.

PART 3

Seven Specific Gifts Of Giving

CHAPTER 10:

THE GIFT OF RANDOM ACTS OF KINDNESS

> *"Do not withhold good from those who deserve it when it's in your power to help them. If you can help your neighbor now, don't say, "Come back tomorrow, and then I'll help you." (Proverbs 3:27–28)*

According to Wikipedia, "A random act of kindness is a nonpremeditated, inconsistent action designed to offer kindness towards the outside world." The phrase "random kindness and senseless acts of beauty" was written by Anne Herbert on a placemat in Sausalito, California, in 1982. Random acts of kindness happen around us every day. From my perspective, these seemingly unexpected actions are usually opportunistic in a good way; the receiver either has a need or is in the right place, and the giver seizes the opportunity.

My Story of Daniel

It was August 8, 1981.

I was seventeen years old and had just graduated from high school two months prior. One evening, instead of waiting for the bus to take me from the train station at 56th and Market Street in Philadelphia, I decided to walk the ten blocks or so home. The walk started pretty normally, and then I saw him—standing on the corner directly in my line of sight.

I remember the confused and frightened look on his face as I got closer. I do not even recall who spoke first, but I know when I approached him, I was not afraid. In his thick, strong foreign accent, he told me his name was Daniel Obai Miller. What came next was enough to make me scared for him too.

He pointed to a house nearby and told me this was the address of a relative he had traveled from Africa to see. I walked the short distance to the front of the house with him hoping to validate whether or not he had the right address. All the visible windows were boarded up, and the house was noticeably vacant. I remember feeling so sad for him at that moment because he was confused, lost, and alone, and he looked even more scared after my confirmation.

At some point, Daniel also told me that after leaving Africa he had a flight layover in New York en route to

Philadelphia. During the layover a few men approached him with the promise of taking pictures of him so he could share the pictures with his family. You know, the typical tourist setup. I wish I could say those particular men had good intentions, but that would be giving too much credit to humankind. Sadly, they stole his luggage and left him with only the few items on his person when we met.

My head was swimming, and my heart was racing. But I knew I could not leave Daniel on this street corner alone to fend for himself—not after what he had experienced in New York and certainly not after realizing he had nowhere to go. So, in my seventeen-year-old grown-up voice, I said something along the lines of everything would be fine. I would just take him home with me, and my mother would figure out what to do next. Simple, right?

I remember the short yet long walk home as I contemplated what to say to my family. Should I start with "Mommy, guess what happened to me on the way home?" Or "Mommy, I'm sorry, but I couldn't just leave him out there!" So instead, I decided to take Daniel to the police station located right around the corner from our house. I left Daniel there, confidently assuming the police would help him.

While the details are foggy after all these years, I decided to go back to the police station the next day only to learn that Daniel was still there. I sprinted back home to tell my mother, and she and a few neighbors followed me back to the police station to see what was going on. After some back and forth, and unsuccessful attempts to reach his relatives and other local resources, my mother very hesitantly decided to let him come home with us.

It was really scary having a perfect stranger in our house that night, never mind someone we could barely understand because of our language barriers. I remember not being able to sleep and wondering how things had gone so far so fast.

My mother said she had never felt fear like that in her life either, yet the alternative of leaving Daniel to fend for himself was unthinkable. I think my oldest brother, Glenn, thought I was out of my mind bringing Daniel home. In our father's absence, he assumed the protective mode and watched Daniel like a hawk. My memory is foggy after that, although I do recall times when Daniel voluntarily cooked meals for us. He still loves to cook and is now a professional restaurant chef. One night, he fried some type of whole fish, and I remember lifting the lid of the pan and being shocked by a big glassy-looking eyeball staring up at me! Daniel gradually assimilated into our family, and we, in turn, learned more about his way of life and culture.

Three months later I enlisted in the United States Army under the delayed entry program. On January 21, 1982, I entered active duty and began basic training at Fort Jackson, South Carolina. Oddly, I had very little contact with Daniel after I left home. It was as if my assignment was over as soon as his life began in America.

Today, my siblings and I consider Daniel our brother, and our mother is his "Mummy." He is our "brother from another mother" who now has biological children and grandchildren of his own from America. Amazingly, our third child, Kiana, and one of his daughters are also friends. With Daniel at the core, we are truly a blended family.

As I look back, my experience with Daniel proved to be the first of many bold and scary opportunities I have had to help others with abandon. Unknowingly, I had passed an important faith test, one that revealed God had my attention when it came to giving, recklessly.

Here are several more recent examples of random acts of kindness that I have either observed or learned about second-hand:

Randy

It was just after 11 a.m. at the Delta Airlines gate. My friend Tracy Leaks and I were heading to the International Maxwell Conference in Orlando, Florida. While we were chattering about a church group Tracy planned to join, we both paused and looked around after overhearing a nearby conversation. Immediately to our right, a tall gentleman dressed in a suit with sneakers—I'll just call him Randy—had just placed a drink tray with three large Dunkin' Donuts drinks on the gate counter. Two of the Delta agents he was looking for were there, but he was looking for a third agent too.

You see, Randy had bought drinks for those three employees either randomly or because he had just had a good customer service experience with them. Tracy and I were surprised yet so delighted to see this random act of kindness unfold before our eyes. Several people around us and on the plane spoke with him afterward, sharing how they also thought what he had done was so kind. To his credit, Randy took it in stride, humbly, as if it were not a big deal and something he did all the time. He was surely a reckless giver.

Cynthia

I met Cynthia at breakfast during a conference. I was telling her and others at the table that I was writing this book and about my motivation for encouraging reckless giving. I looked at her directly after noticing how excited she became, and then she shared this story:

"It was at my work at the time. She was a new hire that I didn't know. I walked through a room she was in when she was telling someone she was homeless and trying to get back on her feet. I offered her my couch in my one-bedroom apartment. She stayed with me until she was able to be on her own. This was about thirteen years ago."

On that very same morning, the woman Cynthia helped

all those years ago left a comment on a Facebook post that Cynthia's husband had written about her. By design or coincidence, the experience was fresh in Cynthia's mind as we sat at the breakfast table. She said she had no idea of the impact her random act of kindness had on the woman until that morning. *"I just have the mindset that when God prompts you to help, you help,"* Cynthia said.

Bruce

My friend Tracy Leaks and I were falling behind a bit for breakfast on the last day of the same conference in Orlando, Florida. We were checking out of the hotel that morning and needed to get our baggage stored so we could move about freely for the remaining sessions. As we approached the down escalator, I hesitated and looked cautiously at Tracy. You see, she had knee surgery five months earlier, and I was pretty sure it would not go well if she tried to navigate the escalator with her large suitcase.

Out of the blue, a man wearing a blue suit jacket came by Tracy's side and offered to take her suitcase down the escalator. He did it so naturally, and as if he did not plan to give her the option to refuse. By the time we all stepped off the escalator, our conversation had already reached a deeper level.

We walked together to breakfast, sat at the same table, and finally formally introduced ourselves. From spouses to children to grandchildren, no topic was off the table (no pun intended) once we got started. It was as if we had known each other for years—kindred spirits meeting and bonding through a random act of kindness.

Ivory

My mother's friend, Ivory, lives in an assisted living facility. One day she went to a grocery store, completed her shopping, and stood in line at the register to check out. Her bill was a little over $100, and she presented her electronic benefit transfer debit card for payment. To her surprise, the transaction was declined due to insufficient funds. She only had a $7 EBT account balance as her current monthly entitlement amount had not been credited yet.

As Ivory prepared to leave the store without the groceries, another woman ran up to her waving a $100 bill. The woman had observed the transaction and, without delay, decided to recklessly help a perfect stranger by paying for the groceries.

Robinson Family

Earlier this year, my grandson had foot surgery. Before his discharge from the hospital, the doctor recommended that he use a knee scooter to get around and to keep the weight off his foot. Of course, his parents immediately called me to discuss doing what grandparents often do best—buying things for their grandchildren. At the same time, they began checking Amazon for prices and delivery date options.

Now, partly because I am a recent semi-retiree and partly because I wanted to avoid buying medical equipment that would only be used for a short time, I told them I would ask a private group on social media whether anyone had a knee scooter in good condition they were not using anymore. I was even willing to pay a discount price for it. Almost immediately, I heard from Pam who lives just around the corner from us. Within the hour I was at her house checking out a practically new scooter that would be perfect for my grandson. As hard as I tried, Pam and her husband refused to accept any money for it. I think from their perspective I was doing them a favor by getting it out of their garage. As we kept talking, I found out the couple has young children, and they are new to Georgia with no relatives nearby. At that moment I felt like God had presented an opportunity for us to help each other as I, in turn, committed to babysitting for them in the future. While I am still waiting for their call, I am grateful for their very timely and random act of kindness.

CHAPTER 11:

THE GIFT OF HOSPITALITY – ROXIE

———◆———

"Trust in the Lord with all your heart; do not depend on your own understanding. Seek his will in all you do, and he will show you which path to take." (Proverbs 3:5–6)

In 2001 my husband David was reassigned to then–Fort Benning in Columbus, Georgia. This military installation has since been renamed from its Confederate name to Fort Moore. David had just completed a tour of duty at the United States Army Reserve Center (USARC) in Macon, Georgia, and we lived just outside of Macon in Warner Robins, Georgia. By then my mother had relocated to the area too.

With his twenty-four years of military service, we looked forward to David's retirement, so he commuted to his new duty station in Columbus while we remained in our home. In February 2003, aligned with our plans to permanently relocate to the metropolitan Atlanta area,

I applied for and was offered a job at a nonprofit agency now known as SourceAmerica—about 125 miles north of Warner Robins.

But then the unexpected happened. By March 2003 the United States and Iraq went to war. Just when we thought we could finally settle down, the Army suspended David's retirement, a term called "stop-loss," and issued him orders to deploy to Iraq. While it was difficult to take, David specialized in logistics, and his expertise and seniority were considered critical for his unit's war operations. Once again we were faced with separation, but this time we had to decide within a very short time whether I would accept or decline my employment offer in Kennesaw. We still had three school-aged children, and we did not want to uproot them as we still expected David would retire soon.

In came yet another blessing—my mother agreed to move in with us and care for our children on weekdays while, this time, both of us were away from home.

On Monday March 3, 2003, I drove from Warner Robins to Kennesaw for my first day of work. By then I had found an extended stay inn near the office, and I initially slept there for two nights. On that Wednesday after work, I drove through the maddening Atlanta-area traffic back to Warner Robins to see the kids, stayed overnight, and then drove back to Kennesaw early Thursday morning. I stayed at the inn again Thursday night and then headed south after work on Friday to spend time with the kids over the weekend.

The plan was to rinse and repeat, and this became my routine until David returned from Iraq three months later.

Somehow one of my co-workers, Roxie Hansen (now Dotson), quickly got wind of what I was doing. Maybe I told her in a passing conversation—I just do not recall. While my timing also might be slightly off, within that first week of my new routine, Roxie invited me to live with her temporarily instead of staying at the inn. I soon found out from her other natural acts of kindness that she is one of the most compassionate people you would ever want to meet.

Now, I do not know about you, but I think it is very rare for someone to welcome a perfect stranger into her home to live without a background check, character witness, or whatever other reputable assurances are available. But then as I began writing this chapter, suddenly I remembered my "brother from another mother," Daniel. Could it be that I was reaping the benefits of what I had sown at the age of seventeen when I brought a perfect stranger to our home in Philadelphia? Although I didn't ask for it or expect it, had God remembered? He did, only this time Roxie gave it back to me *and* my entire family, recklessly.

While I still kept my routine of driving back and forth from Kennesaw to Warner Robins throughout the week, Roxie's generosity ensured I had a stable, clean, and comfortable place to lay my head in between. Knowing how I felt, I am certain the very basic needs of safety and stability are what people experiencing homelessness and living in poverty desire too. That is where we all can fit in and truly make a difference.

As I finalized this chapter, I wanted to finally hear Roxie's side of the story: what she took away from our unique experience and the relationship that began over twenty-one years ago. She was not hard to reach since we still stayed in touch after we retired in March 2023 from the same company where we met. This is what Roxie told me:

> *I remember when you started, and you had that friendly, smiling personality. I heard you were renting a hotel room, and I was in this four-bedroom house all by myself. I thought, "I should just ask her if she would like to stay with me until her house is built." You said "Yes," and there was comfort in having you here. I enjoyed that. Even though you weren't here every single day and you went home on weekends, I knew you were coming back. And I got the nice experience of having the girls come, and I got to know them a little bit. It was like having a little family here. There was not one single time when I wished I hadn't asked you to come here. I was a little disappointed when you left too.*

By far the oddest, scariest, and funniest thing Roxie and I remember about that time happened on April 29, 2003. We were in our separate bedrooms that night, and both of us felt the house shake. Roxie told me at first she thought I was knocking on her bedroom door, so she told me to come in. Then she realized her bed was shaking. I had a similar experience. We both flew out of our rooms and met in the hallway at the same time. Then it stopped. Roxie and I tiptoed down the stairs and opened the front door, and by then several neighbors had come outside too. We were all confused about what had just happened, and Roxie wondered whether it was an earthquake. Later we learned that a small rare earthquake of 4.9 magnitude had shaken the South, and its epicenter was just 160 miles from Atlanta. During our conversation about this book, Roxie also told me she was glad I was with her because the experience was a lot less intimidating than it would have been if she were alone.

As we concluded our conversation, Roxie reminded me that we usually enjoy our blessings or gifts. While she agrees that she has the gift of hospitality, she told me God also gave her a heart to help and care for three elderly people until their deaths. Hospitality and care—no surprises here when it comes to Roxie.

CHAPTER 12:

THE GIFTS OF CARE, ENCOURAGEMENT, AND MENTORSHIP

Jan, Micky, and an Older Gentleman I Observed on an Airplane

"I've learned that people will forget what you said, people will forget what you did, but people will never forget how you made them feel."

– Maya Angelou

Jan Overton

Our immediate family relocated to the Twin Cities in August 1991. In late 1992, after first working at a United States Department of Veterans Administration facility in Minneapolis, Minnesota, I transferred to the U.S.

Department of Agriculture, Agricultural Research Service, which was situated on the University of Minnesota Saint Paul campus. It was there that I had the privilege of working with Jan Overton, the location administrative officer.

Jan was one of those leaders who opened up about professional and personal matters. By her doing so, her staff came to know and appreciate her whole person.

On a personal level, Jan was the reason I started writing family Christmas letters after I saw and admired how she captured what was going on with her family year after year. I began writing them in the mid-nineties, and I am so grateful for now being able to look back and reminisce on the highlights of our children's growth, relocations, vacations, etc. One year I even had several of the letters bound, and then I gave them to my children as Christmas presents. Those letters captured rich family history that we can all look back on and share with generations to come. What a gift!

What I respected most about Jan was how she explained to me and my two co-workers how our jobs fit in the big picture. For example, I understood how my responsibilities as an accounting technician helped her manage the location's budget. She also helped me understand the importance of paying attention to details as I reviewed and reconciled financial information others would use to make important decisions. I watched her extend the same patience to Pam Groth, who was our purchasing agent, and

THE GIFTS OF CARE, ENCOURAGEMENT, AND MENTORSHIP

another co-worker, Mary, who job-shared with me.

Jan was not one of those managers who held information close for her job security. I believe she knew that all of us were important but not irreplaceable because we had other employment and lifestyle options. Through her patience, she taught me that we have to make time and space for people, and we have to give grace and space for people to make mistakes. In her cheerful yet serious manner, Jan always showed us her authentic self and never came off as prideful or condescending in the process.

Another thing I respected about Jan is how she created a work environment that felt like family. On any given day, Jan, Pam, Mary, and I chatted about what was going on in our personal lives, and it felt like a safe place. We each had our personality types, but I cannot recall a single day when we disagreed to the point of being disrespectful or dismissive of each other. I always thought Pam would be Jan's successor, not only because of Pam's overall knowledge of our operations and her relationships with the scientists we supported, but also because I believe Jan had the foresight to understand the organization's future needs after her tenure. With an awareness of those needs, Jan made it a point to share her knowledge, which is a must with good succession planning.

Funny story. One day Jan walked into my office while I was eating popcorn. Now, you have to know Jan to pick up on what her facial expressions mean. As she approached my desk, I recall Jan looking down at the floor with a look of exasperation and disgust, as if I were one of her children who had messed up her freshly vacuumed living room floor. I do not recall Jan's exact words, but her stern, taken-aback expression was enough to let me know she was not happy about the small mess I had made, and that I needed to quickly pick up the stray popcorn kernels strewn across the floor if I knew what was best for me. I still laugh at the memory because, at that moment, I do not think she could have stopped herself from having that very human reaction.

In 1995 our family relocated once again—this time to New Jersey. However, with this relocation I took with me a new perspective on mentorship and leadership. Although Jan might not have known that I was watching and learning from her, she became the first professional person I wanted to "grow up" and emulate as a leader. Also to her credit, the relationships she encouraged and supported in the office still exist today. These are gifts and lessons I have never forgotten.

Micky Gazaway

The gifts and lessons we learn from being mentored, encouraged, or cared for by others can vary based on the givers' experiences and our mindset, situation, and receptiveness, as well as timing. I firmly believe that God introduces certain people in our lives 1) when it is most beneficial, 2) to help us get through difficult personal and professional challenges, and, ultimately, 3) according to His plans for our future. As recipients, we also have to have a willingness to learn from others.

I met Richard "Micky" Gazaway in March 2003. Over the next twenty years, I had the pleasure of working with him both as a subordinate and peer and ultimately considering him my friend. Here are two specific personal memories of his gifts to me and my family that linger.

The year 2003 was very difficult. As I explained in chapter 11 about Roxie, my husband David was deployed overseas for the Iraq War, I had just started a new job in Kennesaw, Georgia, and three of our four children were living with my mother 125 miles away in Warner Robins, Georgia. Our oldest, Demetrius, was in college and lived on campus. Due to the circumstances, I had to commute between Warner Robins and Kennesaw each week. As a new project analyst, I was responsible for managing federal contracts within the agency's southern region territory. These factors provided my first insights into Micky's care and concern for others and his ability to lead.

Technically, I could have been assigned to manage contracts throughout the entire region, which also included US territories. But Micky, as our regional Executive Director, and my two direct managers supported me in receiving a fair volume of contracts primarily within Georgia, Florida, North Carolina, and South Carolina. This allocation allowed me to still perform my job well but without the mental burden of worrying about taking extended overnight trips to contract sites that would have prevented me from seeing my children each week. I do not doubt that my career at the agency would have been short-lived without Micky's leadership, understanding, and support at that time in my life. The same compassion he showed for me resonated so much that I emulated it years later when I too became an Executive Director and had to sign off on decisions that impacted the personal lives of my team members.

Talk about care and patience! One day while I was still a relatively new employee, I brought my nine-year-old daughter Kiana to the office on what used to be called Bring Your Daughters to Work Day. This day is now an annual event in America called the National Take Our Daughters and Sons to Work Day, held on the fourth Thursday in April. Somehow my daughter Kiana got lost, and I was frantically running around our maze of offices trying to figure out where she could have gone. I also checked the bathrooms, kitchen, conference rooms—almost everywhere I could think of, but I could not find her. After exhausting all the practical options, one frightening possibility still loomed: could my bold and courageous daughter possibly have gone into Micky's office? In my head I kept thinking, "No way—she wouldn't dare do that, would she?"

I still remember my fear yet resolute determination as I slowly approached and cautiously tapped on Micky's open door. I overheard what sounded like a fluid conversation and at first thought he was in a business meeting or on the phone. As I craned my neck to the right toward his desk, to my chagrin and horror, I saw Kiana sitting cross-legged in a chair on one side of his desk, while Micky sat facing her looking as attentive as if he were conducting business. I never found out what they were discussing, but I do remember their disapproving looks made me feel like *I* was the one lost, and that I should leave because I was interrupting a very important conversation. Asserting my parental authority at last, I walked fully into the room, firmly grasping and tugging at Kiana's hand while simultaneously mouthing an apology to Micky. At that moment, I honestly didn't know which was worse—being perceived as either a negligent mother or an inconsiderate employee—but Micky quickly erased both those concerns with a pointed stare that assured me everything was alright. Wow. Talk about a lesson in humility and kindness; his response showed me early on that Micky was someone I could trust with the people and things that really matter to me—like my young, inquisitive, and courageous daughter. My other firsthand experiences with Micky abound, but don't just take my word for it. Here are a few other accounts from people who worked with Micky over his illustrious thirty-eight-year career with the organization.

John Bonham

From my experience, there are four words that best describe Micky: giving, kind, calm, and concerned. One day during my first week of working at SourceAmerica, I cut the top of my head in what I will just describe as a very unusual, and hopefully not repeatable, incident. In hindsight I don't know why I thought of Micky first, but I did. As I walked hurriedly into his office with blood running down my face, a blood-soaked towel on my head, and a first aid kit in my hand, I imagined what I must have looked like—flustered, panicked, and clearly out of my element. That is certainly how I felt. As calmly as I could, I asked Micky if he could help me. To my surprise, he immediately stopped what he was doing and gave me his full attention. Next, he asked me to sit down, and then he went about bandaging my head as naturally and carefully as he might have done for someone he had known for a lifetime. Later I would learn that Micky was once an emergency medical technician, and he knew the importance of calming down people first during medical emergencies. Knowing what I know about him today, I don't think Micky's former profession would have mattered much either way because I came to learn that he is the kind of person who sees people in need and doesn't hesitate to try to help.

That same kindness and concern played out over the past year, as Micky and I worked closely together, preparing for his retirement by transferring his Senior Director responsibilities to me. Every day he capitalized on opportunities to teach and mentor me. Another more recent example of his care and kindness, even while wearing his mentor "hat," immediately comes to mind. On that particular day, I was not in a great mood for various personal and professional reasons. With his usual care and kindness, Micky pointed out a couple of situations where my approach to the matters at hand was not ideal. Turns out I did not realize I was exhibiting some counterproductive behaviors that were impacting the team. With his calming approach, Micky explained his concerns in such a way that I was not only receptive to hearing what he had to say, but I also realized I needed to change how I approached and responded to certain situations.

In a nutshell, whether he does it through intentional mentoring or during one-off situations, Micky communicates in a manner that makes people more willing to consider his advice and counsel. This is how he practices giving to others, and he does it in so many helpful, timely ways.

Lawrence Adkins

Since the first day I started with SourceAmerica, Micky made me feel special, and now, almost eight years later, we are still connected in ways that only he and I know and understand. I called on Micky when I needed help, encouragement, or maybe just a conversation. I thank him for listening, and sharing, and for all the days he made time for me.

When I was in the Marine Corps, I had a full-bird Colonel who kind of took me under his wing and mentored me as Micky did, and the Colonel always used a red pen. Since that day (also about thirty-eight years ago), I've always used a red pen. So, at Micky's retirement luncheon in February 2024, I gave him one of my favorite red pens and two cards as a gesture from the bottom of my heart. As a mentor, friend, and incredible leader, Micky made a difference in my life. I will always cherish and remember our personal and professional relationship.

THE GIFTS OF CARE, ENCOURAGEMENT, AND MENTORSHIP

Asya Kouyoumdjian

I wrote this to Micky in an Easter card:

I just wanted to share with you how grateful and appreciative I am to you! You have become a good example of a true leader for me—the one who does know his job very well but, most importantly, genuinely cares for those entrusted to him. I keep praising and thanking God for you and for how richly He blessed me through you. I pray that the Lord bless you even more than what you could ask or desire for!

I know many others would willingly share similar sentiments about Micky. When I asked him whether he was aware of his positive impact on so many people, Micky responded in his usual unpretentious manner. To paraphrase his perspective, he is just a man who learned early on from one of his great mentors the importance of taking care of people. That lesson and his innate authenticity meshed with his Southern upbringing where, although he did not grow up with people of diverse backgrounds, he came to understand the value each person can bring to the table if given the opportunity.

An Older Gentleman I Observed on an Airplane

On a flight back to Atlanta in 2022, I sat behind and across the aisle from an older gentleman. What I first noticed was the legal pad with pages full of notes he appeared to be studying. Next, typed notes from a manuscript of sorts had his attention. As we got closer to landing, I looked over again and saw the gentleman reading a book. As he read, he used a pencil to underline sentences that resonated with him.

Something about the gentleman's posture and focus reminded me of someone … the metaphorical light bulb came on as I smiled and realized that someone was me! His reading pace slowed as he deliberately took time to study and underline text. I thought to myself, "Man, at the rate he's going, when will he ever finish reading that book?!" Despite our descent for landing, he showed no signs of rushing through the material.

It occurred to me then that, despite his apparent age, this gentleman is a lifelong learner. As he finally reached down to gather his old tattered brown leather satchel to put away his precious reading materials, I imagined he could easily have been an educator or tenured professor.

Whatever his past or present profession, that older man taught me something that day through his intentionality and focus. I left that flight reminded that personal growth and learning should never stop until we die. There is always something new to learn and someone new from which to learn.

And as we learn, we never know who is watching—our kids, grandchildren, *or even someone sitting behind and across the aisle from us on an ordinary flight.* In those moments, knowingly or unknowingly, we have yet another opportunity to give by modeling lifelong learning. The examples we set can cause others, especially our youth, to evaluate or reevaluate their perspective of personal and professional growth just like that older gentleman did for me that day on a flight back to Atlanta.

CHAPTER 13:

THE GIFT OF CANDOR– DAVID AND JACQUI

David Nelson

I have a deep respect and appreciation for my husband David's generosity toward others. Since I met him over forty-one years ago, I have seldom witnessed a time when he did not prioritize or make a sincere effort to help family, friends, and even strangers in their times of need.

Sometimes, however, we also need to hear the raw truth from those who are genuinely concerned for us. It takes a special kind of person to communicate with others authentically, in a manner that not only gets to the heart of a matter but also leaves us with hope and a promise of continued support and encouragement as we walk through the peaks and valleys of life. That type of candor is what I have observed year after year from David.

Since my husband comes from a very large family, he has many nephews and nieces. His nephews in particular reach out to him frequently for advice about life in general, work, and cars. I know they see David as a role model, particularly because he follows through on commitments and has a way with words that leaves no doubt about his opinions and sincerity. To the person, they know when they call him, they will get a response. Listen to what four of David's nephews said when I asked what they appreciate most about him:

Dana Pearson

"He's giving, loving, and wise in all situations."

Carlos Woodard

"A real '100' man, uncle, friend. A person that is going to be there when you need someone to talk to and count on."

Jesiah Bickford

"Unk David is a stand-up guy, a man of his word. He's a leader, loyal to the soil. A mentor and most importantly he never forgot about me or left me out. When we have our little talks, his words cut through to [me] every time."

Deion Bradley

"It's more than just a few things. I appreciate his persistence and dedication toward the family and his patience and understanding. His love is unconditional. He has faith in me even when I don't have faith in myself. He leads by example with consistency and high expectations that he reaches and gives me an idea of how to do my very best just by showing me it's possible. He understands that I'll always be his nephew, and he pushes to make me understand that. He always comes home too. Uncle David doesn't let money distort his relationship with or views on a person even if they owe him. He tries instead to better their situation with help getting a job or at least looking for one for them, and he normally just wants a call sometimes. That's an amazing person in a selfish and shady world. Nobody's like Uncle David. He's my hero. My Master Sergeant Uncle. Uncle David reaches out the most if I'm not in Georgia. He doesn't give me a choice [with laughter]. You guys can take credit for a majority of the reason I have a chance in this world because of the military, especially you."

Jacquelyn "Jacqui" Sheridan

"Some people make cutting remarks, but the words of the wise bring healing." (Proverbs 12:18)

Out of all my friends I have written about, Jacqui's story took the longest to pull together. I cannot clearly explain why that was the case, other than it required me to think about the best way to articulate how her personality, sensitivities, and wisdom blend when she uses her gift of candor to help people.

Firstly, Jacqui is an empathic listener and effective communicator. I am sure she honed these skills during her extended careers in the retail and banking industries where one is measured by her ability to dig deep to find out what people want or need. On a personal level, I have watched Jacqui use those same skills to counsel and support young people in and outside of her family. She tries to get to the point quickly so people can move on to solutions.

The sensitive side of Jacqui shows up in her laughter or tears, and sometimes both in the same conversation. I just love how she leans into conversations through her facial expressions and by looking intently into people's eyes. If it is a funny topic, she can burst into teary, loud, hearty laughter within the blink of an eye. As I will share in chapter 16, Jacqui and her husband, Parrish Sheridan, have mastered the art of evoking belly laughs, especially when you are in a conversation with them together. During touchy-feely or serious conversations with Jacqui, you can see and hear her transform into the nurturing, supportive person she is.

Jacqui also embodies Proverbs 27:17, which proclaims, *"As iron sharpens iron, so a friend sharpens a friend."* Whenever I have called or gone to Jacqui over the last twenty-five years or so about a deep personal matter, I always knew she would give me her best—whether through sound counsel, encouragement, or a much-needed reality check.

Because we have never had a specific conversation about what I see as her spiritual gift of candor, I reached out to Jacqui to hear her perspective. This is what she told me:

> *When I speak with people the way I do, it really comes from the heart, and I never do it with intent to harm. Yes, I am a straight shooter and candid. Even right now I'm tearing up just thinking about the tough love I have for people, or whatever people want to categorize it as. It comes from a good place. I would also hope someone loves me enough to give it to me straight, without offending me,*

just like the Bible talks about speaking truth in love. I can take the tough stuff too. Over the years I have learned to be able to take the feedback because anything we hear, God intended for us to hear it. When you're led by the Spirit, we know in this world things will hit you differently. It's also a maturity thing; we can't always absorb things when they initially happen. I hope that people can see and understand what God intends to do with those experiences.

At this point in our conversation, I told Jacqui about an older woman at the church I attended in Minnesota who once told me I needed to learn to say "No." When I was around the age of twenty-seven, she saw me volunteering in multiple capacities in the church while juggling my responsibilities as a wife, mother, and employee. At the time I did not fully understand or appreciate her critical words when I otherwise thought of her as a warm, loving person. Years later I finally understood the love behind her words and have since had similar conversations with younger women.

Some of Jacqui's closing words in our conversation surprised me but also came with a welcome challenge: *"It's been a privilege to have our friendship, but I also think we need to have some deep conversations that we haven't even broached. When we do, I wonder what aha moments we will have. Is there going to be a learning curve to build our bond even closer? I am honored and humbled that you reached out to me, and I hope this book does what you intend for it to do."*

CHAPTER 14:

THE GIFT OF BELONGINGNESS–IDA AND JAIDA

―――◈―――

Ida Williams

    I could dedicate an entire book to my sister-in-law, Ida. In it I would try to get personal testimonies from everyone she has helped to any extent since I met her forty years ago. I would aspire to interview the many children, teenagers, and young adults she has taken into her home, the relatives she "found" and introduced to the rest of the family, and all the relationships she helped bridge with her wisdom. But that would still not be enough. You see, Ida's generosity extends not only to the gift of belongingness, but also to the food, money, clothing, and encouragement she lavishly and sometimes sacrificially gives to those in need.

    When I spoke with Ida's youngest daughter, Ebony Haugabrook, she was so excited about sharing how her mother's giving has affected her life. She said if she had to categorize what she experienced and observed, her mother's generosity would fall into one main bucket: sowing faith.

You see, when Ebony was growing up, Ida introduced her to God, but not directly. What Ebony went on to explain is so like the sister-in-law that I know and love: always thinking about what is best for others in the long run. This is her account:

> *When I was growing up, my mother was not a "church person," but she understood the value of church and knowing God. She made sure I, and my two siblings, were surrounded by people like our Aunt Bren to get us involved with the church. My mother also made it her business to maintain a relationship with Aunt Bren—who is my cousin's aunt, not my biological aunt—because she knew she could trust Aunt Bren to keep us involved in church activities. Essentially, through their strong relationship, my mother positioned us so that we would always be in the right environment to learn about Christ.*
>
> *On some Saturdays we would stay overnight at Aunt Bren's house and go to church with her the next morning. Sometimes my mother would drive to the church on Sunday mornings, look for Aunt Bren's car in the parking lot, and then drop us off for service*

because she knew Aunt Bren would take care of us when we arrived. She also knew Aunt Bren would either bring us home afterward or allow us to hang out with her until all the day's services were over. My mother was also a faithful giver. She always gave us offerings for church, sometimes a $100 bill. That was the beginning of us going to church, learning about Christ, and understanding the importance of giving.

Whenever we spent the night at our dad's house, my mother would show up early to take us to church. Our dad didn't push us because he was not a churchgoer either. If we told him we did not want to go, he would take our side and tell her we didn't want to go. Most times she completely ignored him and would take us home anyway to get dressed and then drop us off at church. Eventually, my dad knew she meant business, so he had us dressed and ready when she arrived. Amazingly, years later my dad became a whole pastor himself! God would have it that he started attending church faithfully and went from serving as a deacon to becoming the church's pastor.

The bottom line is that my mother knew the importance of establishing faith in her kids early on, even though she did not attend church. Being in the church led to me hearing about Christ over and over, and certain principles just stuck. The seed was planted; my faith became a foundation, a roadmap for how I move today. I also prayed to God about the type of husband I wanted—one with good character, a certain style with clothes, etc. My husband didn't have a style with clothes when we met (at least to my preference), so every year I would buy him items to build his wardrobe. But all that mattered was his heart. We have now been married seventeen years and have three wonderful sons that we are also bringing up in the church.

Collectively, my Aunt Bren and my dad's churches built my Christian foundation and contributed to who I am today—full of faith! That's why when I got married, I asked my Aunt Bren to walk me down the aisle instead of another blood relative. I remembered her generosity when she used her gas to get us around town even when she was on a tight budget. She had two jobs and was barely making it. Yet she sacrificed to take care of me and my siblings—physically, emotionally, and spiritually. It's the kind of generosity I will never forget.

One of Ida's nieces summed up Ida this way, which I believe also complements Ebony's description of her mother: loyalty to a fault, strong work ethic, and a jack of all trades. She is also a confidant, always ready and willing to listen and give advice based on her experiences and acquired wisdom.

When I think about the various ways we all can give, Ida sets the example when it comes to unifying family and sacrificially giving so that others can have better opportunities in life.

Jaida Anderson

> *"You watched me as I was being formed in utter seclusion, as I was woven together in the dark of the womb. You saw me before I was born. Every day of my life was recorded in your book. Every moment was laid out before a single day had passed." (Psalm 139:15–16)*

Children do not ask to be born into this world. Perhaps like you, I have heard and repeated this controversial phrase countless times. While it sounds trite and unappreciative, especially coming from the mouth of an unhappy teenager, at the core of this statement is an undeniable truth. At conception, children truly do not get a vote. That decision ultimately rests with our Creator and the man and woman who become their biological parents. Also, while the circumstances surrounding conception might vary, Psalm 127:3 teaches us that in all cases, *"Children are a gift from the LORD; they are a reward from him."*

According to a 2021 report cited by USAFacts.org, over 600,000 children passed through the United States foster care system over one year.[9] While studies show an overall decline in the number of children in the foster care system over the last two decades, children who remain in the system and ultimately age out tend to be more vulnerable to criminal activity, poverty, and homelessness, and they are at greater risk of living their lives alone.

While the foster care statistics are grim, thankfully there are also many instances of individuals and families who have submitted to God's imperative to care for their relatives as we find in 1 Timothy 5:8: *"But those who won't care for their relatives, especially those in their own household, have denied the true faith. Such people are worse than unbelievers."*

Let me share with you yet another example of reckless giving that I have watched unfold over the past fifteen years.

Patrice truly loved her three children—Deandra, Calvin, and Khalia. But no matter how hard she tried, substance abuse and mental health problems gripped her relentlessly. Time after time Patrice reached out to her older sister, Jaida, to bail her out. When she just needed to get away for a while to clear her head, which usually meant hanging out without the encumbrances of her children, Patrice could always rely on Jaida to take them in. That is, until the year her addiction got so bad that the court system stepped in and gave her an ultimatum: either complete the recovery program and stay clean for good, or lose her parental rights and the children would be placed into foster care. After multiple painful attempts at rehabilitation, it became clear that Patrice was no longer capable of parenting her children.

Jaida and her husband had only been married a few years when they agreed to initially take temporary custody of the three children. Despite the newness of their covenant relationship, the young couple's strong belief in God and deep concern about the alternatives left no room for inaction. By then Deandra was eight, Calvin was six, and Khalia was three years old. According to Jaida, watching the pain, turmoil, and back and forth the children experienced was too much to bear. She says Jeremiah 29:11, one of her favorite Bible verses, also affirmed God's divine purpose and plan for each of them: *"'For I know the plans I have for you,' says the LORD. 'They are plans for good and not for disaster, to give you a future and a hope.'"* This Scripture became the young couple's call to action, as they realized their responsibility to be an integral part of the children's hope and future.

Today, Deandra, Calvin, and Khalia are thriving young adults. Yet who but God knows what their lives would have been like if Jaida in particular had not yielded her heart to recklessly love and provide for her sister's biological children like God recklessly loves and provides for His own every day? As Christians we know, or should know, that God does not promise a life without struggles or doubt when we submit to His purpose and plan for our lives. However, if we remain faithful and rely on Him all along the way, He does promise to see us through.

> *"That's why I take pleasure in my weaknesses, and in the insults, hardships, persecutions, and troubles that I suffer for Christ. For when I am weak, then I am strong." (2 Corinthians 12:10)*

CHAPTER 15:

THE GIFT OF TIME – KIMBERLY

Our youth are our future. Without a doubt our nation's future prosperity, stability, and security will depend on the instilled values, norms, and social and emotional well-being of today's youth. What an exciting, provocative, and sobering thought!

Now more than ever, our youth must be surrounded by people who encourage and are willing to listen, guide, and impart wisdom. To be effective, those same people must be personable and relatable so that youth feel comfortable opening up and sharing their deepest thoughts and aspirations. Finally, and most importantly, they must also be trustworthy; from a biblical perspective, I believe trustworthiness includes ensuring any spiritual gift we use aligns with the word of God.

My sister-in-law, Kimberly Nelson, has given to the

youth in our family in this way. Not that we are discussing animals, but she reminds me of a horse or dog whisperer—you know, those people who have the innate ability to calm wild horses or understand how a dog is feeling or thinking. In her special way, Kimberly uses her spiritual gifts to connect with young people, which has noticeably benefited multiple generations in our families.

As I mature, I am learning the importance of acknowledging my feelings, assessing the root cause of any feelings that are not pleasing to God, and then making a concerted effort to turn away when or if I have thoughts that bring me back to those unpleasant feelings. Follow me with this thought. When God gives others unique spiritual gifts—such as Kimberly's gifts of her time, and her ability to encourage and connect with youth—we should step back and let it happen, especially when we do not have the same gifts. While I love to sing, I know my "lane" does not extend beyond the confines of my car, the bathroom, or other places where I am completely isolated from others! I do not think I have a horrible voice, just not one that I am comfortable using in front of others.

Consider also what God's Word says about our unique gifts. In 1 Corinthians 12:4–6 the apostle Paul tells us, *"There are different kinds of spiritual gifts, but the same Spirit is the source of them all. There are different kinds of service, but we serve the same Lord. God works in different ways, but it is the same God who does the work in all of us."* This dying world needs people like Kimberly to help our youth. But if as a parent or guardian, you are inclined toward jealousy or feelings of inadequacy when another Godly person speaks into your teenager's life, consider the alternative. Would you rather your teenager cultivate a relationship with someone you do not know or trust? If your teenager is in crisis or needs an immediate word of encouragement, who would you rather she turn to if you are not available? If your relationship with your son is less than ideal, would you rather he turn to someone you can trust or someone who is a bad influence? The scenarios abound.

I believe when God blesses us with the responsibility of parenthood, He also knows we will occasionally need help. We cannot always be on our game. We do not always have the patience, knowledge, or even the time to unpack every kind of situation our children might experience. I encourage you today to be that parent or legal guardian who recognizes your human limitations but especially God's omniscience and omnipotence. How can you do that without totally abdicating your parental authority? I believe it starts with surrounding your children with the right influences, like Kimberly, and then gracefully stepping back when you encounter situations that might best be approached by someone other than yourself. Satan might counter that doing so somehow detracts from your parental rights and responsibilities or unconditional love for your child—but we know he is a chronic liar and the truth is never in him. Pray first, and then give yourself the gift of simply letting go while God does through others what only He can do.

Interestingly, Kimberly told me that she never really thought about her gift in the way I described it, but she sees how it all connects. From her perspective, she has simply always wanted to be available to stand in the gap for family members. She rightfully views herself as a trusted counselor who willingly gives sound guidance and encouraging words to our youth. I believe hers is a beneficial gift that every family needs.

CHAPTER 16:

THE GIFT OF ENDURING FRIENDSHIPS

"The truth is, no matter how lonely you might feel, you're never going through anything alone ... you can choose your family."

– Jennifer Lopez

We were about a block away from the restaurant where David said we were having dinner when, oddly enough, I saw one of our nephews walking rather quickly down the sidewalk and in the same direction my husband and I were traveling. Frankly, I could not imagine why this very sociable thirty-something-year-old man, whose uniquely styled hair locs made him stand out in a crowd, would want to frequent any place in this historic Marietta, Georgia, neighborhood. It was also an early quiet evening, and he lived a considerable distance away. Perhaps it was my imagination, but it also looked like our nephew gave my husband a sidelong, secretive glance that reluctantly acknowledged he had been seen. Still rather puzzled, I asked David what he thought our nephew might be doing in the area. My husband paused and mumbled a few incoherent words, so I chalked it up to coincidence.

I vividly remember David pulling into a lot with several other parked vehicles, stopping near a historic-looking house, and getting out of our car. I also saw one or two other familiar people who scurried quickly inside the building. As you might imagine, my radar was on full alert by then as we slowly climbed the short flight of stairs toward the foyer. Within a few steps, I entered the large room in front of me and instantly froze. The sea of faces in front of me took my breath away as I simultaneously heard them shout, "Surprise!"

At that moment it was almost impossible for me to reconcile the mosaic-like picture in front of me. Why were so many of my friends like Theresa, Avis, Jacqui and Parrish, Qunnie and Calvin, Thad and Jackie, Christina and Charles, and Henrietta and Willie all together in the same room? Never mind my brother Michael, our four children, and a host of other relatives who were also there. My head swirled as I tried to make sense of the incredulous picture in front of me.

You see, I had met each of the friends I mentioned, and the families they represented, during various seasons of my adult life. Somehow, as we traveled from place to place over the years, I had compartmentalized these relationships into buckets of time. Like Rudyard Kipling's ballad, I imagined, "Oh, East is East, and West is West, and never the twain shall meet …"[10] Now, it was not that any of these friends would be purposely rude or discourteous to each other like the ballad implied; it just felt odd and disjointed that they were all there in the same room—staring back at me—as if it was always part of a bigger plan.

When I was finally able to shake off my initial shock and take in the surroundings, I realized it was *my* surprise fiftieth birthday party! And, by what I define as a divine miracle, all those beautiful people had sacrificed their precious time to come love on and celebrate *me*. Ten years later I still reminisce about that momentous occasion. Most importantly, I thank God continually for the families He surrounded us with when we needed them the most—those who could and could not attend my party. Here are my accounts of many of those life-changing relationships.

Memories Relived

> "Women's friendships are like a renewable source of power."
>
> **– Jane Fonda**

I met Theresa Dawson (now Woods) and Avis Ross (now Chatman) in June 1982, only seven months after enlisting in the Army. We were assigned to the same military company

GIVING, RECKLESSLY

at then–Fort Hood, Texas; lived in the same barracks; and worked in the same office as administrative specialists. Coincidentally, I also met David in June 1982, and he was in the same military company too. As you might guess, we all became friends.

By the way, while I will continue to refer to then–Fort Hood in this chapter, this military installation was renamed on May 9, 2023, to Fort Cavazos in honor of General Richard Edward Cavazos. General Cavazos was the Army's first Hispanic American promoted to the rank of a two-star brigadier general in 1973. In 1982 he became the first Hispanic American four-star general while he commanded III Corps at then–Fort Hood, Texas.[11] Interestingly, our military unit fell under his command while we were stationed there.

Avis, Theresa, and I have so much rich history. We applied for our first retail credit cards together, have children of similar ages, and even made it a priority at one point to exchange important phone numbers of our respective family members so we would never lose touch. Sort of like a pinkie swearing oath, but at a much older age. Talk about secrets—oh, boy, those two know a lot of mine!

In the early days of our friendship, it was quite common for young soldiers to spend their paychecks on frivolous items and end up with more month than money. They would then pawn items, like furniture and jewelry, to get enough money to hold them over until the next payday.

Payday loans with high interest rates were easy to get, and many soldiers also pawned their car titles to hold them over. These predatory pawn shops and unscrupulous car dealerships lined the main streets of Killeen, Texas, just outside the military installation. I believe many businesses preyed on the abundance of young service members who came through their doors every day, because many of us were away from home for the first time, and we lacked money management skills. We knew we were "grown," we received regular paychecks, and we did not have to ask our parents' permission to spend money we earned.

Sadly, I fell victim to one of those shady deals too. In 1983 I purchased my very first car in Killeen—a 1977 yellow and white Ford Pinto—for about $1500, if I remember correctly. I learned much later that this was the same model car that received heavy media and government attention because the fuel tanks ruptured after the cars were rear-ended. Tragically, this flaw, while comparable to other 1970s subcompact cars, resulted in several deadly fires. Surely a lemon law or some type of disclosure was in order, but the car dealer did not tell me anything. I know now that I should have done some research too, but I cannot help but believe the sale was just one more unscrupulous transaction with a young and naïve female soldier like me.

I still laugh whenever I think about my friend Theresa threatening to throw away a large Curtis Mathis floor-model television that I bought from a pawn shop for our barracks room. When I walked into the room, she was ready to charge with a defiant look and both hands on her hips. She had decided the TV took up too much space and that either I or it needed to go. Perhaps it was our mutually resolute, pointed stares at each other that eventually broke the tension, because the showdown ended fairly quickly. We worked it out, and to this day, we still occasionally laugh about that disagreement. Theresa and her small family relocated from then–Fort Hood to Germany in early 1983; what we did not anticipate was about six years later we would come together again after my family relocated to Germany too.

Avis was, and still is, the great athlete of our trio. Her physical endurance and calm during difficult situations are truly enviable. Impressively, Avis is one of only two female friends who has consistently exercised since I have known her. In her subtle and caring way, she still encourages me to stay active. Avis was reassigned from then–Fort Hood to the country of Belgium in late 1984, but we committed to staying in touch. How our paths intertwined afterward could only be described as providential.

In 1985 I received military orders for Fort Belvoir, Virginia, in a new career field of topographic surveying. If you have ever observed new commercial construction or bought a newly constructed home, surveyors are the people with tripods who measure and assess the land and then feed that information to developers and cartographers. A far cry from my initial military job as an administrative specialist, I know, but the change brought with it career advancement.

But I digress.

By then David and I were married and had one son, Demetrius. In mid-1986 Avis completed her overseas tour in Belgium, received an honorable discharge, and moved back to her hometown of Arlington, Virginia. Turns out Arlington is only about twenty miles from where we lived in Lorton, Virginia, a city just outside of Fort Belvoir. Avis told me at some point after she returned home from overseas, she reached out to my sister, whose phone number she had kept in an old personal phone book. Our plan to keep the numbers of each other's family members in case we lost touch worked, and my sister gave Avis my then-current phone number. Even then God was setting the stage for His next timely blessing that would unfold over the next two years.

I was honorably discharged from the Army in May 1987 about eight months after our second child, Tiffany, was born. Before my discharge I also began experiencing some medical challenges that ultimately resulted in a diagnosis of rheumatoid arthritis. Over the next four years, this inflammatory autoimmune disease stealthily worsened and led to additional complications that I described in chapter 7.

In 1988 David received military orders for Frankfurt, Germany. Unfortunately, the children and I had to remain in the States until overseas military family housing became available. By then I had met most of Avis's immediate family, but I never expected her sister, Gina Ross, to invite me and the kids to stay with her for a short time while we simultaneously planned a temporary move to live with my Philadelphia family until we could join David. Although her apartment was small and she also had a young son to house and feed, Gina recklessly and compassionately offered practical strangers the interim housing stability we needed. Even as I recount this tumultuous chapter in my life, I cannot help but remember again my non-biological brother Daniel and how we first met seven years earlier in Philadelphia. It is true; God has a perfect memory, and He repeatedly blesses those who bless others.

Even as I recount my friendships, I would be grossly remiss if I did not mention how my sister and her family supported me and the kids when we temporarily relocated to Philadelphia after living with Gina. Thanks to their kindness, we had a place to stay, and to this day, my son Demetrius has fond memories of his kindergarten grade school experience in Philly. Not only did her family take us in, but they also introduced us to neighbors and looked out for our overall welfare while we lived in the city.

By May 1989 our small family of four was together again in Frankfurt, Germany. That is where we met James and Danetta King, Calvin and Qunnie Parker, and their respective children. Collectively, this set of friends became our family away from home during one of our most challenging and frightening military assignments.

You see, just before Christmas in 1990, my husband deployed to Kuwait for Operation Desert Shield. By then Demetrius was seven years old and Tiffany was four. They did not understand what was going on, and in my effort to keep things normal, I suppressed my fears about David's well-being and the increasing tension that loomed all around us. Military spouses learn quickly how important it is to maintain stability within the family during hardship separations. When you factor in a war or other military conflict, it becomes increasingly important to keep things as normal as possible for the children.

James and Danetta were an Air Force family, and Calvin and Qunnie were an Army family like us—but neither of the military husbands in these families deployed. Trust me when I say that I could write chapters about the love, friendship, fellowship, and compassion these special people extended to our young family as we endured the five-month separation from David. We watched each other's children, attended the same church, and shopped, ate, and celebrated birthdays together. Our children went to the same elementary school, sang together in our church choir, and forged strong relationships that still exist today. We also comforted and assured each other in that volatile overseas environment as war protests, bomb threats, armed soldier barriers, and car searches in our housing area were the daily norm. King Solomon described our relationships best with his words in Proverbs 17:17: *"A friend is always loyal, and a brother is born to help in time of need."*

GIVING, RECKLESSLY

On a more humorous note, I remember Calvin once saying that Qunnie, Danetta, and I could always find excuses to go shopping at the commissary or base exchange store even when we didn't need a thing. Since there was an inkling of truth to his assertion, we just laughed and let him off the hook. To me, certain friends have privileges, and he was one of them.

Even then Qunnie inspired me by her bold proclamations of faith in God. Fast forward to the present, and her steadfastness and ministry work remind me of the Titus 2 woman who embraces holiness and reaches back to help younger women live wisely and not disgrace the word of God.

James and Danetta gave me my first insight into the lives of Air Force families. I began calling him "Brother James" back then, and I was so thankful for his sense of humor. Sometimes I would call their house, and when James answered, I would jokingly disguise my voice to sound like a man and ask him if my girlfriend Danetta was home. Corny as they were, those brief conversations brought me levity during some difficult times. Danetta and I were very close, and she got me acclimated to the nuances of the surrounding Air Force bases like Rhein Main where we also attended church. One of my most memorable experiences with her was a ride we took on Germany's high-speed highway system, called the Autobahn. She was driving in the far-left lane and got particularly annoyed by a driver who was following too closely behind us. Danetta started putting on the brakes in spurts to hopefully get the driver to back off so we could change lanes. Although her strategy eventually worked, it was a very frightening experience.

Almost thirty-five years later, I am happy to share that my family still enjoys rich, inseparable relationships with the King and Parker families. We cherish the memories and will never forget that season when God showered us with His bountiful gift of protection.

After yet another separation and temporary relocation to Philadelphia for me and the kids, our entire family arrived in Minnesota in 1991. Frankly, the Twin Cities of Saint Paul and Minneapolis were never on our list of places where we wanted to live. However, after carefully weighing other less favorable options, like Hawaii and its high cost of living, David received orders for Fort Snelling Army Reserve Center in Minneapolis, Minnesota. By this time, eight-year-old Demetrius and five-year-old Tiffany were both in elementary school. As you might imagine, we were grateful to find and rent a townhome in a friendly neighborhood with lots of other children for our kids to befriend.

We learned very quickly that two of the most predictable things about the Twin Cities are massive snowfall and sub-freezing temperatures. At least from our experience, snowstorms are fair game from as early as September through the end of April. Do you remember how I described my winters in Philadelphia, particularly how much I enjoyed the snow? Well, my friend, snowfall in the City of Brotherly Love barely compares to the Twin Cities experience.

I loved watching history repeat itself as our children played with the neighborhood kids just as hard as I had many years before. There was one particular slope across the street from our townhome that gave them so much joy. They would use makeshift sleds like cardboard boxes to glide down that slope—that is, until one of the children hit a tree and split open his lip pretty badly. The kids also jumped rope, played tag, and got into all kinds of age-appropriate trouble just like me and my childhood friends. It was amazing! I was about twenty-seven years old then, and I vividly recall occasionally racing my children at top speed through the neighborhood. And guess what? I always won!

Not only were we blessed to have our third child, Kiana, in Minnesota, but we also developed more family-like relationships there too. Several of the people we bonded with were military families, and others were not. Some of these friendships have stood the test of time, while others did not.

My friend Juliet Wiley (now Mitchell) was there for me then, and she is still one of my biggest champions. I still remember how she encouraged me to take exercise classes at 5:30 a.m. almost daily at the local gym—something I needed after all the weight I gained during my pregnancy. In the mid-nineties, step aerobics classes became very popular, and we loved the structured yet rhythmic movements up, down, over, and across the steps because it kept us in great shape. Also, our sons were the same age and attended the same school, so we spent even more time together as their friendship grew.

Many years later in 2017 when our youngest daughter, Mikhala, began a college internship at General Mills in Golden Valley, Minnesota, I made it a priority to let Juliet know our baby was coming her way! Even though she had never met Mikhala, Juliet quickly assured me that she and her husband were just a phone call away if she ever needed anything. When Mikhala went on to become a full-time General Mills employee a year later, words cannot describe my relief knowing that although we would be a thousand miles away in Georgia, my good and trusted friend was nearby.

After I started Pivotal Connections, LLC, in 2021, Juliet sent me these kind words, and I used the last sentence of it as a testimonial:

> *I have known Leslie for over twenty years! Wow! Little did we know that our connection through our kids (children) would result in a long and strong relationship. The core of our relationship is what has helped to sustain our connection through the years:*

love and commitment to family, service to the community, and supporting young people. When I think of Leslie, the picture is clear: loving, kind, supportive, intelligent, poised, and professional.

Fast forward to 2023: I and many of Juliet's family members and other friends celebrated her sixty-fifth birthday in grand style. I continue to be blessed by the gift of this friendship that has also stood the test of time.

While she also did not make my fiftieth birthday celebration, I cannot forget my friendship with Keisha, whose kids and nephews were joined at the hip with my kids when we lived in Eagan, Minnesota. From our children's jaw-dropping sled rides down nearby hills to the never-ending elementary school activities, I cherished the time we shared with them. Several other friends in Minnesota warmed our hearts, and we are so grateful to have known them.

In 1995 we drove our family and household goods over 1,200 miles from Minnesota to our next duty station at Fort Monmouth, New Jersey. We lived in military family housing in the surrounding city of Eatontown. In case you are wondering why we decided to drive so far with three children who were around twelve, nine, and two at the time, one of the reasons was the financial incentive the military offered. Driving also allowed us to visit family and friends along the way. Our relocation overseas to

Frankfurt, Germany, was the only time we did not choose a "do-IT-yourself" or DITY move—not that we could have driven there anyway. As you might imagine, packing and unpacking our household goods ourselves and then putting our house back together each time we relocated took quite a bit of energy, which also meant I had to delay starting work until we were settled in. While I have talked about the dynamics of military life in other chapters of this book, the toll of moving is one aspect of military life many people do not understand or realize occurs with military families. The sacrifices of military service extend to each family member as they continually leave behind relationships, careers, and short-term stability.

We developed many more friendships in New Jersey. While I will not describe each relationship in detail, our collective family remembers and thanks them for helping us make it through yet another challenging military assignment. Not long after we arrived, we joined Calvary Baptist Church in Red Bank and met Parrish and Jaquelyn Sheridan. She goes by Jacqui for short. At first, I had no clue the two were married. While we met them at the same church, they served in different ministries, so I never saw them in the same place together. One night I went to Bible study at what I thought was only Jacqui's apartment. It was only a block or two from our military housing. I remember looking rather confusingly at a picture on the wall because I simply could not understand why they were in the picture together. Sure, Parrish was also at the Bible study, but their relationship still did not register in my mind. As the night went on, they eventually introduced themselves as a married couple.

While I generally avoid comparing people and relationships, Parrish and Jacqui have given to my family in more ways than I could ever articulate. As a couple, I mostly love how each of our adult children still relates to them and respects their points of view—including their longstanding faith in God. While they became Tiffany's official godparents, unofficially they parented each of our children in one way or another. We trusted them implicitly to impart spiritual wisdom and truth when we were not around.

But there is even more to their story. I have watched over the years as Parrish and Jacqui have positively impacted and influenced many other young people with their candor, patience, and resources. I specifically wrote about Jacqui's special gift of candor in chapter 13. Talk about belly laughs: when I need a comedic "fix," they are my go-to couple. Finally, over the years Parrish and Jacqui not only welcomed us into their lives but also introduced us to many of their extended family members.

It was Sunday June 23, 1996. Because of my chronic medical condition, lupus, my obstetrician scheduled the exact day I was to deliver our fourth child. David had not made it to the hospital yet, and I waited restlessly in my hospital bed for him and my medical care team to arrive.

THE GIFT OF ENDURING FRIENDSHIPS

Our friend, Thaddeus Spencer, who later became a pastor, is someone I will just refer to as an aspiring comedian. This man can reduce you to tears if you even crack the door open for his contagious sense of humor to meander in.

As I sat propped up in that hospital bed, imagine my surprise-turned-to-laughter when Thad swaggered into the room carrying the most pathetic bouquet of weeds. You heard me right—weeds! Knowing him, I knew it was a spontaneous gesture to bring some levity to the situation, and it worked. We got a bigger laugh—actually, one of those "Eww!" moments—when the medical team walked in and addressed us as husband and wife. Turns out our daughter Mikhala was not born until the next day, but that funny yet thoughtful scene with Thad was just one of many memories that make him so special.

Looking back, I do not recall exactly when I first met Thad and his beautiful wife, Jackie. I do know David met Thad, who was an active-duty Army officer, at Fort Monmouth, and our families eventually connected through our church and extracurricular activities. But I think what sealed our relationship was the immediate connection between their two loving children and ours. Many times when David was away, this amazing family showered us with love, companionship, and genuine care. Jackie recently retired from a career as a teacher. I am certain many of her students benefited from her wisdom, commitment, and kindness toward them. She is a jewel! The gift of Thad and

Jackie's friendship runs deep, and I cannot imagine what our lives would have been like without them.

Although they could not make my milestone birthday celebration, God also blessed us by letting us know Paul and Francine Saffold, Robert and Patricia Williams, Willie and Diane McQuay, and their respective children, who mostly made up the rest of our New Jersey nucleus of friends. These were people we also forged strong relationships with as we laughed and cried together through highs and lows, celebrated family achievements, worshipped in church together, and cared for each other in ways that I will never forget. Whenever Francine, Thad, and Parrish were in the same room, we were guaranteed to experience their unique rendition of an amateur comedy show. More times than not, the trio made me laugh until I cried.

Our family's next relocation landed us in Warner Robins, Georgia, in 1999 when David was reassigned to the U.S. Army Reserve Center in Macon, Georgia. While David would complete two additional assignments in Iraq and then–Fort Benning in Columbus, Georgia, our family did not physically move again until late 2003 in anticipation of his retirement the following year.

I developed so many more memorable, lasting relationships while we lived in Warner Robins. Angela Williams, Cheryl McClendon, and Leslie Lake are just a few of the people whose friendships I appreciate and cherish to this day, not to mention the countless friendships our children enjoyed.

Angela Williams's gifts to me have always been her wisdom and level-headedness that encouraged me through two major career shifts, my first and current entrepreneurial journeys, and those inevitable spiritual battles. She is a gracious, kind, and beautiful woman who faithfully lives out God's command to care for brothers and sisters in need. It is so wonderful to see where she is today: in her late sixties not only still lovingly caring for her elderly father but also enjoying travel with her daughter and the devoted love of her son.

While Cheryl and I grew apart in later years, I still remember how close we were in those days. We laughed a lot together, participated in church ministries, and supported each other through some very difficult personal experiences. Cheryl always had a flair with her clothes and hairstyles that made her look so … jazzy! Her children and my two oldest, Demetrius and Tiffany, enjoyed special friendships too.

Finally, there is Leslie Lake. As you might imagine, sharing the same first name helped with our initial connection. He is a longstanding deacon at the church we attended, and we both worked at Robins Air Force Base as federal government employees. When my mother also moved to Warner Robins and joined our church, at some point Leslie became her deacon too. Almost twenty-five years later, two of Leslie's most treasured gifts to me are the kindness and care he still extends to my mother from afar. He is a complete package with his melodious Jamaican accent, infectious laughter, and singing antics that somehow all manage to reinforce the sincerity of his heart and how important people are to him.

Do you remember my Army friends Theresa and Avis, whom I befriended in 1982? Well, soon after my family permanently relocated from Warner Robins to the metropolitan Atlanta, Georgia, area in 2003, Theresa introduced me to one of her sisters who also lived there. I remember feeling as if Theresa had invited me even further into her family circle, and that she had not forgotten our commitment to stay connected with each other's families. When Avis's father died in 2018, Theresa and I were right there in the rear church pews silently sending our prayers and comfort forward to our grieving friend. Similarly, when my father died in 2021, Avis and her sister Gina traveled from Northern Virginia to Philadelphia for his funeral. Grief had me in a mental fog that day, but my mind cleared up long enough to see my sweet friend Avis. Over forty-one years later, we still prioritize calling each other at least once a month. Avis, her sister Gina, and I also vacationed together in December 2023.

Avis told me recently that it is so hard to develop authentic relationships these days—especially with people you can just call up to say how you are feeling and share what is going on in your life. She said we need people we can trust and know they will listen. So, with the true friends you have, you have to value and trust those relationships. I completely agree with her.

In chapter 6, "By Design or Coincidence," I mentioned my friend Henrietta in an example of fundamental attribution errors. But I recall first seeing Henrietta at a PTA-sponsored event at our daughter's elementary school about twenty years ago. She immediately impressed me with how she related to people and took charge. Our friendship grew after we officially met while serving in the children's ministry at our church. Little did I know then that a bonus for forming a friendship with her would later be to befriend her future husband, Willie Smith. And who but God would have known that he would get his realtor license just in time to represent my husband and me as we relocated from Virginia to Georgia and purchased a new home in 2021? I think we would all agree that it is wonderful when we have the pleasure of working with proficient professionals in any industry; high-fives to God for positioning Will to work with us because we knew and trusted him too. When our daughter Tiffany began exploring the field, Will was also right there encouraging her until she became a realtor and got her real estate license. Not surprisingly, God's timing in both situations was flawless!

Christina Conley and I became friends around 2008 when she also began working in the children's ministry at our church. The greatest gift she has given me in our long relationship is the example of boldly declaring God's Word over matters we experience. As a recently retired educator,

Christina uses what I believe are her gifts of discernment and artistic expression to help me and others understand not-so-obvious biblical truths. Inspired by 2 Corinthians 9:10, Christina started Seams Sewn, LLC, through which she meticulously and thoughtfully creates quilts that capture the most tender, significant, and celebrated memories of her customers' lives. We also share common experiences of military life: Christina's husband, Charles, retired from the Air Force after twenty years of service. I love hearing how the two now gleefully immerse themselves in the blessings of grandparenthood. As God has called them to do, they make room for their beautiful grandbabies in their home and lives.

Because we moved so frequently, we met many, many other people whom I have not mentioned. My intention was not to minimize the significance of any of those relationships but to allow my heart and spirit to revel in the diverse blessings God sent me through them all.

I'll end this chapter by sharing that I often reflect on why leaving home at the age of seventeen was one of the best decisions I have ever made—even though I did not know it at the time. Secondary to meeting my husband and raising our beautiful family together, God gifted me with incredible lifelong friends who were there at the very beginning and who continue to enrich my family's lives today. That mind-boggling truth also reminds me of a January 2024 sermon by Pastor Broderick Santiago (affectionately known as Pastor B.), senior pastor of Mosaic Church in Mableton, Georgia.

According to Pastor B., in our lives we have people who are "Day Ones" and others who are "One Days." While the latter group will always cross our paths, deep relationships with them are often just hopeful and mainly elusive. On the contrary, Pastor B. told us we can identify those who have our backs and will continue to stick with us by four characteristics. Specifically, our "Day Ones" …

1. Do not just want to see you win, but they help you win. Read Philemon in its entirety, and Philippians 4:17–19.

2. Are the right people to help keep you upright. Read Galatians 2:11–13.

3. Hold you up when you are going down. They pick you up where you have left off. Read Exodus 17:8–13 (especially verse 12).

4. Are not in your life seeking blessings; they see being in your life as a blessing.

Thank you, God, for all my "Day Ones." I count all of these personal relationships as more in a series of Your benevolent, incredible gifts to me. You have blessed me beyond measure with friendships that have stood the test of time.

> "The best gift anyone can give, I believe, is the gift of sharing themselves."
>
> **– Oprah Winfrey**

EPILOGUE

As I conclude this book, there is one aspect of my marriage and the act of giving that did not quite fit into any of the previous chapters. I think it is important to share it at this point because it summarily reinforces how our childhood and other life experiences can hugely impact the degree to which we give to others.

In chapter 5, "On the Receiving End of Giving," I was very candid about the childhood experiences that shaped my desire to give. Turns out my husband, David, often shares with me tidbits about how poor his family was too when he was growing up. At times something we are doing or observing triggers those memories. He was raised in southern Georgia primarily by his late mother, Effie Cleo Lott-Shine. Mom Effie had seven children, and she worked very hard to keep the family fed, usually by holding multiple subservient jobs to make ends meet. I still laugh whenever David talks about plucking and eating so many pears from trees in the neighborhood when he was growing up that he hates the mere thought of eating a pear now. Then there were the countless arguments he and his siblings had about food, like who was able to craftily grab and eat the last portion. Truth be told, I am not so sure those incidents were not just excuses to give each other a hard time—as most siblings tend to do.

Interestingly, in our forty years of marriage, we have never sat down to intentionally talk about *why* giving is so important to each of us. We are also that fairly odd couple that has never worked from a combined family budget, although we mutually agree to pay our household bills on time, maintain good credit, invest, and save money—albeit not necessarily in that order. I also know that David comes from a place of sincerity and kindness when he helps others.

Many times I hear about his gifts to others—in many forms, not just financially—after the fact. For example, David has a propensity for helping people with flat tires or other mechanical car issues. Our close family members and friends all know that some of his greatest joys in life are troubleshooting car issues and taking apart and putting together old used cars. Along those same lines, many times he told me after the fact how he helped motorists, mainly females, who were stranded on the side of a road. I am sure being a husband, father of three girls, and uncle to many nieces plays a big factor in his desire to help in this way too. He would not want any of us stranded in our cars without any hope of someone stopping to help.

Admittedly, I give to others in ways that David is not aware of too. While some might argue we should make all financial decisions together, we are extremely comfortable using our discretion based on the situation at hand. While we do not always agree on the extent of each other's giving,

EPILOGUE

there has never been a time when our separate decisions negatively affected our family's financial security, or when we did not ultimately yield to each other's ability to decide.

So here's my final point.

We are all spiritually gifted in one way or another. Many people have multiple spiritual gifts. The full discovery of those gifts might come at different times or through different assignments, as we *all* go through the stages of conception, gestation, and birth within the metaphoric wombs of our lives—female and male alike.

I want to encourage you to explore what God has given you uniquely without comparing yourself to anyone else. Once you discover your gifts, ask God to help you understand how to use them effectively according to His will. Finally, open your arms wide and watch in wonder as the doors of opportunity burst open to reveal an incredibly exciting and fulfilling new way of living. *Embrace it, submit to it, and trust that this new way of living is our Father's divine demonstration of His form of reckless giving.*

APPENDIX 1:

ADDITIONAL BIBLICAL SCRIPTURES AND QUOTES

Chapter and Verse(s)	Scripture (All New Living Translation)
1 Chronicles 29:11	"Yours, O Lord is the greatness, the power, the glory, the victory, and the majesty. Everything in the heavens and on earth is yours, O Lord, and this is your kingdom. We adore you as the one who is over all things."
Proverbs 2:5–8	"Then you will understand what it means to fear the Lord, and you will gain knowledge of God. For the Lord grants wisdom! From his mouth come knowledge and understanding. He grants a treasure of common sense to the honest. He is a shield to those who walk with integrity. He guards the paths of the just and protects those who are faithful to him."
Proverbs 3:9–10	"Honor the Lord with your wealth and with the best part of everything you produce. Then he will fill your barns with grain, and your vats will overflow with good wine."
Proverbs 11:25	"The generous will prosper; those who refresh others will themselves be refreshed."
Proverbs 18:23	"The poor plead for mercy; the rich answer with insults."

Chapter and Verse(s)	Scripture (All New Living Translation)
Proverbs 21:13	"Those who shut their ears to the cries of the poor will be ignored in their own time of need."
Proverbs 21:26	"Some people are always greedy for more, but the godly love to give!"
Proverbs 21:27	"The sacrifice of an evil person is detestable, especially when it is offered with wrong motives."
Proverbs 21:30	"No human wisdom or understanding or plan can stand against the Lord."
Proverbs 22:2	"The rich and poor have this in common: The Lord made them both."
Proverbs 22:9	"Blessed are those who are generous, because they feed the poor."
Proverbs 22:16	"A person who gets ahead by oppressing the poor or by showering gifts on the rich will end in poverty."
Proverbs 22:22–23	"Don't rob the poor just because you can, or exploit the needy in court. For the Lord is their defender. He will ruin anyone who ruins them."
Matthew 9:36	"When he saw the crowds, he had compassion on them because they were confused and helpless, like sheep without a shepherd."
Luke 6:36	"You must be compassionate, just as your Father is compassionate."
Luke 12:31	"Seek the Kingdom of God above all else, and he will give you everything you need."
John 13:35	"Your love for one another will prove to the world that you are my disciples."

APPENDIX 1

Chapter and Verse(s)	Scripture (All New Living Translation)
2 Corinthians 5:21	"For God made Christ, who never sinned, to be the offering for our sin, so that we could be made right with God through Christ."
2 Corinthians 9:6–8	"Remember this—a farmer who plants only a few seeds will get a small crop. But the one who plants generously will get a generous crop. You must each decide in your heart how much to give. And don't give reluctantly or in response to pressure. 'For God loves a person who gives cheerfully.' And God will generously provide all you need. Then you will always have everything you need and plenty left over to share with others."
1 Peter 4:10	"God has given each of you a gift from his great variety of spiritual gifts. Use them well to serve one another."

"Grant, O God, that we may follow the example of your faithful servant Barnabas, who, seeking not his own renown but the well-being of your Church, gave generously of his life and substance for the relief of the poor, and went forth courageously in mission for the spread of the Gospel; through Jesus Christ our Lord, who lives and reigns with you and the Holy Spirit, one God, for ever and ever."

– **C.S. Lewis, British writer**

"The true leader serves. Serves people. Serves their best interests, and in doing so will not always be popular, may not always impress. But because true leaders are motivated by loving concern rather than a desire for personal glory, they are willing to pay the price."

– **Eugene B. Habecker, Author**

APPENDIX 2:

ADDITIONAL REFERENCES AND RESOURCES

"2 Corinthians 9 | The New Testament Daily with Jerry Dirmann (April 24)." YouTube. April 24, 2023. Video, https://www.youtube.com/watch?v=iMN4k88uHOo.

Corbett, Steve, and Brian Fikkert. 2012. *When Helping Hurts: How to Alleviate Poverty Without Hurting the Poor ... and Yourself.* 2nd ed. Chicago: Moody Publishers. www.moodypublishers.com.

Desmond, Matthew. 2006. *Evicted: Poverty and Profit in the American City.* 1st ed. New York: Broadway Books. broadwaybooks.com.

Haupt, Angela. "Yes, You Can Get Better at Saying No." *TIME.* November 16, 2023. https://time.com/6332017/how-to-say-no-better/.

Kozol, Jonathan. 2006. *Rachel and Her Children: Homeless Families in America.* 2nd ed. New York: Three Rivers Press. www.crownpublishing.com.

Lester, Terence. 2019. *I See You: How Love Opens Our Eyes to Invisible People.* 1st ed. Downers Grove: InterVarsity Press. ivpress.com.

Smith, Timothy L. "10 Examples of Generosity in the Bible and How to Follow Them." Crosswalk.Com. January 11, 2024. https://www.crosswalk.com/church/giving/10-examples-of-generosity-in-the-bible-and-how-to-follow-them.html.

APPENDIX 3:

OUR MILITARY ASSIGNMENTS AND/OR SIGNIFICANT EVENTS TIMELINE

Year(s)	Military Assignments and/or Significant Events
1977	David began active-duty Army service with his first permanent duty station in Wiesbaden, Germany.
1981	David was reassigned to Fort Hood, Texas.
1982	Leslie began active-duty Army service with her first permanent duty station in Fort Hood, Texas, where we met.
1983–1984	David was reassigned to Seoul, Korea, for a one-year hardship tour. Our son, Demetrius, was born. We married. David was reassigned to a second tour of duty at Fort Hood, Texas.
1985–1988	David and Leslie were reassigned to Fort Belvoir, Virginia. Our daughter Tiffany was born. Leslie received an honorable discharge.
1988	David was reassigned to Frankfurt, Germany, without family. The family initially remained in Virginia followed by a temporary relocation to Philadelphia, Pennsylvania.
1989	Our family was reunited with David in Frankfurt, Germany.
1990	David deployed to Kuwait for six months in support of Operation Desert Shield while the family remained in Germany.

Year(s)	Military Assignments and/or Significant Events
1991–1995	David returned from Kuwait and was then reassigned to Fort Snelling, Minnesota, with family. Our daughter Kiana was born.
1995–1998	David was reassigned to Fort Monmouth, New Jersey, with family. Our daughter Mikhala was born.
1998–1999	David was assigned to Kuwait for a hardship tour. The family stayed in New Jersey until he returned.
1999–2001	David was reassigned to Macon U.S. Army Reserve Center, Macon, Georgia, with family. We resided in Warner Robins, Georgia.
2001–2003	David was reassigned to then–Fort Benning, Georgia, in 2001, then deployed to and returned from the Iraq War in 2003.
2004	David retired after twenty-seven years of military service.

ENDNOTES

[1] "The 7 Forms of Generosity." Trinity Family Wealth Advisors, n.d. https://trinityfamilywealth.ca/the-7-forms-of-generosity-2/#:~:text=There%20are%20seven%20forms%20of%20generosity%3A%20Thoughts%2C,words%2C%20money%2C%20time%2C%20things%2C%20influence%2C%20and%20attention.

[2] Keller, Timothy. 2008. *The Prodigal God*. 1st ed. Penguin Random House LLC. penguinrandomhouse.com.

[3] Scholes, Peter. "They'll Know We Are Christians." Hymnary.Org, January 1, 1966. https://hymnary.org/text/we_are_one_in_the_spirit.

[4] Fischer, John. "Reckless Giving." The Catch, October 18, 2018. https://catchjohnfischer.live/2018/10/18/reckless-giving/.

[5] Lewis, C.S. 1952. *Mere Christianity*. 1st ed. The Macmillan Company.

[6] Charles Studd Quotes. BrainyQuote.com, BrainyMedia Inc, 2024. https://www.brainyquote.com/quotes/charles_studd_167357, accessed May 6, 2024.

[7] Taylor, James, & Carole King. "James Taylor & Carole King – You've Got A Friend (BBC In Concert, 11/13/71)." YouTube, February 26, 2021. https://www.youtube.com/watch?v=nEFfzHiEKHY.

[8] Dickens, Charles. 1859. *A Tale of Two Cities*. 1st ed. Chapman & Hall.

[9] "How Many Kids Are in Foster Care?" USA FACTS, August 23, 2023. https://usafacts.org/articles/how-many-kids-are-in-foster-care/.

[10] Kipling, Rudyard. "The Ballad of East and West." The Kipling Society, January 1, 1889. https://www.kiplingsociety.co.uk/poem/poems_eastwest.htm.

[11] "Fort Hood Redesignated to Fort Cavazos May 9." U.S. Army, May 9, 2023. https://home.army.mil/cavazos/index.php/about/fort-cavazos-redesignation.

Printed in the USA
CPSIA information can be obtained
at www.ICGtesting.com
LVHW010432230824
789004LV00009B/189